It's Not About the Shark

ALSO BY DAVID NIVEN, PH.D.

The 100 Simple Secrets of Happy People
The 100 Simple Secrets of Successful People
The 100 Simple Secrets of the Great Relationships
The 100 Simple Secrets of Happy Families
The 100 Simple Secrets of the Best Half of Life
The 100 Simple Secrets of Healthy People
Simple Secrets for Becoming Healthy Wealthy and Wise
100 Simple Secrets Why Dogs Make Us Happy
Up! A Pragmatic Look at the Direction of Life

It's Not About the Shark

HOW TO SOLVE
UNSOLVABLE PROBLEMS

David Niven, Ph.D.

St. Martin's Press ✒ New York

www.stmartins.com

Design by Patrice Sheridan

Library of Congress Cataloging-in-Publication Data is available upon request.

ISBN 978-1-250-04203-3 (hardcover)
ISBN 978-1-4668-3923-6 (e-book)

St. Martin's Press books may be purchased for educational, business, or promotional use. For information on bulk purchases, please contact Macmillan Corporate and Premium Sales Department at 1-800-221-7945, extension 5442, write specialmarkets@macmillan.com.

First Edition: November 2014

10 9 8 7 6 5 4 3 2 1

To Tina and Katie

Contents

It's Not About the Shark

Problem or Godsend?

THE PRESSURE ON the young director was unrelenting.

He had burned through the studio's money and exhausted their patience.

After shooting was finished each day, the knot in his stomach grew tighter and tighter as he screened the new footage with his team. Sometimes they would watch an entire day's work without finding anything that could be used. "Frankly, the more we saw, the more we worried," recalled Bill Butler, the film's cinematographer. "We had *a problem*."

It wasn't hard to identify the crux of the matter. The film's star, playing the title character, was simply impossible to work with. Complicating matters, the usual inducements—money, flattery, obsequious attention to his comfort—had no effect whatsoever on the film's fickle lead.

So day after day, Steven Spielberg sat in the dark, watching another reel of another day's wasted footage. He was directing his first movie for a major studio. He had already heard the whispers of doubts from studio executives, worried that he was in over his head. He had already overspent his film's *entire* original budget on one prop. He was rapidly becoming convinced this would not only be his first film but his last.

More to the point, though, he had to face the reality that the mechanical shark he had cast in a starring role in his film *Jaws*, a shark he imagined haunting moviegoers' dreams as some kind of Godzilla of the sea, couldn't swim, couldn't bite, couldn't even tread water.

It was not for lack of effort. The shark—nicknamed Bruce in honor of Spielberg's lawyer—was a phenomenally complicated pneumatically powered colossus, attached to 150 feet of hose linking it to compressors floating above, on a barge. It took a small army of people—each working a different lever that controlled a fin, or the eyes, or the mouth—to make it go. It had been designed by the most experienced talent in the industry—people credited with creating the giant squid in *20,000 Leagues Under the Sea* and some of the most frightening sea creatures ever to appear on film.

But, to an almost comic degree, the shark was a failure. Originally tested in a freshwater tank in California, the shark was shipped to the Massachusetts coastal town where the movie was to be made. There, the filmmakers received a crash lesson on the uniquely corrosive effects of salt water. As its controls shorted out, the shark would move or not move without the slightest interest in who was pulling which lever. Every day there was something else that needed to be repaired, replaced, or re-welded because it didn't work or had been damaged during filming on the rare days the shark had been functioning while the cameras were on. Even its synthetic skin failed, as it became waterlogged and bloated, transforming the terrifying shark into a giant sea marshmallow.

"It kept failing and failing and failing and failing," said Bill Gilmore, one of the film's producers. Richard Dreyfuss, who played an oceanographer in the film, vividly remembers getting into position to start shooting a scene, only to hear the relentless squawking of the crew's walkie-talkies and the alarmed words that rang out from them repeatedly: "The shark is not working . . . The shark is not working."

Even on its best day the shark was loud and slow. "You could get out of the water, dry off, and eat a sandwich before it could get you," said *Jaws* cameraman Michael Chapman.

Millions of dollars, months of time, the best technical experts they could find, and what Steven Spielberg had was a rapidly closing window to make a movie about a shark . . . and no shark.

With a broken-down great white shark on his hands, Spielberg had a great big problem and several unattractive options. He could put all available resources into repairing the shark—and almost certainly see his unfinished movie shut down when he ran out of money and time. He could ditch the failing shark and start from scratch, building a new version designed to overcome the first model's limitations—and almost certainly never gain the green light to resume filming. He could forge ahead with the malfunctioning shark, employing translucent wires or whatever tools he could improvise to make it move—and get the film shut down, get himself fired, or make a laughably bad movie, consigning his film and his future to the realm of *Attack of the 50 Foot Woman* and other movies remembered only for being embarrassingly bad.

This is a book about what we do when we have a problem. And research shows that what we do most of the time is crawl deep inside our problems. We define everything on the problems' terms. We limit what we think is possible based on the boundaries the problems set for us. We look at the problems every which way, only to conclude that every available response produces alternate forms of failure. Like staring at the sun and not being able to see the sky all around it, we stare at our problems and cannot see anything else, much less a solution.

Steven Spielberg did not stare at his problem.

Despite the fact that the script began with a close-up view of the shark attacking a swimmer, and despite the fact that the shark was featured all over his storyboards throughout the movie, Spielberg took the failure of his mechanical shark as an opportunity to reimagine what he was doing. He didn't think of ways to tinker with the broken shark or plead for more time and money that would not have been offered—instead, he flipped the situation on its head.

"I thought, 'What would Alfred Hitchcock do in a situation like this?'" Spielberg explained. "So, imagining a Hitchcock movie instead of a *Godzilla* movie, I got the idea that we could make a lot of hay out of the horizon line, and not being able to see your feet, not being able to see anything below the waistline when you're treading water. What's down there? It's what we don't see which is really, truly frightening."

From that thought he saw the solution: Make a shark movie *without the shark*.

Spielberg supplied the suggestion of the shark—in the sight line half above and half below the water, in the ominous and unforgettable John Williams score (which he described as the sound of unstoppable force). And that suggestion of the shark provided the unmistakable, unrivaled presence of menace.

Instead of being the center of every scene, the shark does

4

not make a full appearance on screen until eighty-one minutes into the movie. "It became, the less you see, the more you get," Spielberg said, "because that invited the audience to come to the movie bringing their collective imaginations, and their imaginations helped me make that film a success."

"He had to invent, on the spot, another way of shooting," Richard Dreyfuss declared admiringly, "which was to *imply* the shark, which made an ordinary film into a great film."

Audiences and reviewers were awed by the effect. Calling Spielberg a gifted director, the critic Frank Rich hailed his originality, noting that "the most frightening sequences in *Jaws* are those where we don't even see the shark." Audiences made *Jaws* the highest-grossing film to date and inspired Hollywood to build their year around the summer blockbuster. Its reputation has only grown over time; it has been named one of the greatest films of all time by the American Film Institute, and it's become one of a small handful of films permanently preserved by the Library of Congress as a cultural treasure.

All this from what the studio originally saw as a minor league horror movie—a second-tier endeavor behind its top priorities that summer, the forgettable and long since forgotten *Airport 1975* and *The Hindenburg*.

This is a book about problems, but more importantly, it is a book about solutions. The science, you will see, is spectacularly clear: If we look to our problems first, if we let a problem define the entirety of what we do next, more likely than not we will fail. If we set our problems aside and seek solutions, we can succeed beyond all limitations. In fact, fixing the problem itself becomes a side note in a story of a much larger accomplishment.

You know, nobody ever asks Steven Spielberg why he couldn't come up with a better shark.

It all seems so very simple—and yet focusing on solutions is a profoundly elusive path that runs counter to all our life's lessons. Everything we have ever been taught, every native impulse we have, every source we turn to for help has made us believe that when we have a big problem, we should focus our time, energy, and attention on it, we should work harder, dig deeper, and fight the problem with everything we have. And if Steven Spielberg had done that, his shark and his film would have sunk straight to the bottom of the sea.

Through the science and stories of real people facing real challenges, you will see that whatever your problems at work, at home, in life may be, you can solve them if you are willing to look for a solution instead of staring at the problem. And when you do that, the problem won't be so scary anymore. After all, as Steven Spielberg put it, "The shark not working was a godsend."

Chapter 1

- - - - - - - - - -

Imaginary Philip and the Problem of Problems

WHAT IF THE bumblebee knew it couldn't fly?

We all know what would happen: He'd sit around worrying about how fat he is, and he'd never get off the ground again.

But there's another side to that story. In 1934, when entomologist August Magnan concluded that flying bumblebees defied the laws of physics, he never bothered to tell the bees. And they kept right on flying.

Problems infect our thinking in many ways—but the basic equation is simple. If we let problems define who we are, if we let problems serve as our guide, then our problems tell us what we can't do. We can't do this. We can't do that. Our lives become negatives and absences.

A problem, no matter how important, no matter how significant to our well-being, doesn't belong in the center of our thoughts.

A problem is a barrier. We thrive as thinkers, as doers, as

people when we take barriers down. Think about any great advance in any field of endeavor: a great thing, a great idea, a great product, a great story, a great cure. That greatness came about because somebody brought down a barrier. A problem is a barrier. You have to bring it down, or it will bring you down. Just like the bees.

THE ODDSMAKERS LABELED him a 300-to-1 shot. Which is a polite way of saying he had no chance of winning the tournament. But the rookie golfer Ben Curtis was just glad to be there, having barely snuck into the field by qualifying two weeks earlier.

There were good reasons for the modest expectations. As he teed off at the 2003 British Open, Ben Curtis had never won a professional golf tournament. In fact, he had yet to finish among the top 25 at any event. Curtis even shared the oddsmakers' views of his abilities. He was there for the experience, he explained, to have fun and to try to get better by playing against the best players on one of golf's toughest and most famous courses.

Still, the joy of a small-town Ohioan incongruously standing on golf's brightest stage delighted fans and commentators. Their delight was eclipsed only by their shock as Ben Curtis sank his 8-foot putt on the 72nd hole and hoisted the famous Claret Jug as the winner of the British Open.

How improbable was his victory? It had been ninety years since any golfer had won the first major tournament he had entered.

In the space of a weekend, everything changed for him. An

anonymous golfer who had never won anything, Ben Curtis now stood beside the kings of the sport, living out what he admitted was a "fairy tale come true." He had to clear time on his schedule to visit the White House, because the president wanted to congratulate him personally. And among the many prizes afforded the winner of a major championship in golf, he collected something of the sport's golden ticket—a champion's exemption that allowed him to pick exactly which tournaments he wanted to enter for years to come.

By 2011, that champion's exemption had expired. Worse, it had been five years since Curtis's last win on the PGA Tour, and he was playing just to hold on to the status of a full-time professional golfer.

Curtis was desperate to stay on the tour. And the desperation shaped his game.

"Every time I walked onto the course I thought to myself, 'OK, how am I not going to have a disaster?' " he said.

His sole focus on each hole was avoiding mistakes. "Out there, I'm trying to do everything I can to not make bogeys and double bogeys," he said. "That's what my game has become."

The effort to avoid mistakes clearly had an effect: He made more of them.

"What I was doing, the way I was thinking, was adding more pressure on myself," Curtis said. "More pressure you don't need."

Worse, he was carrying his mistakes from one hole to the next. "In my head I would see replays of a bad tee shot two holes later. I would think about a missed par putt on the next green," he said. "Even when I had opportunities to put up a good score on a hole, I would think of ways I might make a mistake."

Staring at the problem left Ben Curtis stuck—exactly where Steven Spielberg would have been if he had kept his focus on his rotting mechanical shark. Fortunately for Curtis, he finally hit bottom.

At the end of the 2011 season, having failed to win or even contend for a title, Curtis's standing on the PGA Tour was reduced to conditional status. He would, in effect, need to ask for special permission from the sponsors of golf tournaments to let him play anywhere in 2012.

Each week he sat by the phone, hoping to hear that the tournament director had picked him from among the 50 or 100 players asking for one of about eight late-entry slots into the tournament. Most weeks, the phone didn't ring.

But something happened to him on those weeks when he did get into a tournament. Suddenly, the pressure was gone. Because he had no status to protect, the prospect of a bad round didn't scare him so much. He began to just play golf again.

Four months into the 2012 season, playing in just his fourth tournament of the year, Curtis ended a winless streak that had stretched out over more than 2,000 days. His win in the Texas Open restored his full-time professional status and, more importantly, reminded him of what he was capable of doing.

"Golf is that way," he said. "It will come up and surprise you if you let it."

You are an advanced engineering student. Your class is about to be given what amounts to a pop quiz. In a moment, you'll be asked to sketch out designs for a product.

You rub your hands together in anticipation. Whatever the task, there's no doubt you'll come up with something great.

You smooth out your paper and keep your drafting pencil close at hand.

You're asked to come up with a bicycle rack to mount bicycles on a car. You are given various requirements, but the most important objective is to make a rack that is easy to attach to the car and easy to mount bicycles on.

You are shown an example of an existing but inefficient roof-mounted bicycle rack. It has metal tubes running across the car's roof. Into the tubes, a bicycle's tires are secured. It is, you are told explicitly, very difficult for users to secure the tubes to the roof of the car. Meanwhile, the center tube is nearly impossible for all but the tallest and strongest users to access.

You are asked to come up with as many designs as you can that meet the requirements. You have an hour. Now get to work.

You think about bicycles and cars, their shapes and sizes. You think about people having to lift their bicycles and secure them.

You didn't become an engineer to be mediocre. You're not trying for a merely acceptable design. You are there to be the best. So you put pencil to paper and get started.

You can do anything within the parameters of the task in terms of materials or shapes or approaches. So you spin the paper around to get a look at things from a different angle. Your pencil starts flying.

But one image keeps coming to mind. That roof-mounted rack with the tubes. The one with the flaws.

Your first sketch looks just like it. So does your second. Try as you might, your designs keep coming back to roof-mounted tube racks—ideal if your customer base is comprised of NBA centers.

What you didn't know is that at the same time you were creating variations of that failed design, another group of engineers in the next room was also drawing up plans for bicycle racks.

The only difference is that they were never shown the picture of the bad design. And they were never told to try to avoid putting bikes in the middle of the car's roof. They were just told to come up with the best design they could.

When researchers David Jansson and Steven Smith lined up all the designs from your group, and all the designs from the other group, the differences were enormous. The group that saw the bad example came up with fewer total designs, far fewer original approaches, and was much more likely to wind up with bikes mounted where no one could reach.[1]

It wasn't that the second group was any more talented than the first. They weren't. It wasn't that the second group knew anything more about bicycles or bike racks. They didn't.

The difference between the two groups was just this—the first group was asked to solve a common problem with bike racks, and they flailed against the challenge. The second group was asked to design the best bike rack they could, and they did. In the process, they solved a problem they didn't even know existed.

Jansson and Smith repeated their experiment with other challenges and other engineers, and each time the same thing happened. When asked to design a measuring cup for the blind, the majority of engineers shown a design problem couldn't solve it. More than 80 percent of the group that wasn't shown the problem solved it without even knowing what they were up against. When asked to design a spill-proof coffee mug, those shown the design problem with the mug were seventeen times more likely to fail than those who weren't shown the problem.

These were all very talented engineers. All knowledgeable, capable, skilled, and driven. Yet their likelihood of succeeding varied tremendously based on what they were trying to do. The group that had never seen a bad example let their natural talents carry them to a good design. They wasted not a moment on the problem and spent all their time on the solution. The group that saw the problem wanted to solve it so badly they couldn't think straight. Just like Ben Curtis couldn't golf when he was focused on his flaws, these engineers couldn't design when focused on the problem. But they stayed focused on the problem because problems are so seductive and compelling. It is hard to think about anything else.

"People who don't hate their jobs, they just look at you with dread, like what you have is contagious and they don't want to catch it," Michael observed.

"Or, they say, 'Hey, suck it up, it's eight hours of your day, you can survive it,'" he added. "But the problem with hating your job isn't so much the eight hours you're there, it's the other sixteen."

Just like all those engineers who wanted to fix the bike rack problem, and just like Ben Curtis's fear of bogeys, Michael's problem consumed his entire field of vision.

"Because when you hate doing something, it's all you can think about," Michael said. "When you're at work you count the minutes until you can leave, but right when you leave you think about how you have to go back again. Sunday's just the day before you have to go back there."

Michael knows many people have the same frustrations. "A lot of people are bad at their jobs, right?" he said, "But try being bad at your job in front of an audience."

Teaching five sections of algebra at a community college meant thirty-five or so witnesses every time Michael stood at the front of the room, struggling to hold anyone's attention. He knew the formulas, could recite them backwards and forwards, could probably teach this stuff in his sleep. Unfortunately, his students weren't learning much in theirs.

"I didn't get sleepers every day," he said. "Some of those once-a-week night classes—with the double period—wow, I would probably lose half the class by the end. And I don't think they were dreaming of polynomials."

It wasn't just a feeling that Michael was underwhelming in his work; there was ample evidence. "We use a common final exam across the college, to test how much progress everyone is making, or, for my students, not making." Michael's students consistently ranked fourteenth, fifteenth, or sixteenth out of groups of students taught by sixteen instructors. And the student reviews of his teaching were not exactly encouraging. One student said that they should use Michael's classes as an interrogation technique—forced to sit through one of his lectures, any bad guy would crack and confess.

"The worst part of all this is that I care," Michael said. "I care that my students do well, I care that my classroom be a place where math comes alive instead of where math goes to die."

So Michael did what almost anyone in his situation would do—he tried hard to get better. He read every article and book he could find on great teaching. He watched videos on teaching techniques. He went to every teaching workshop on campus and flew to teaching conferences across the country.

"By the time I finished being taught all I could find about teaching, I wound up trying just about everything and then trying to undo it. I sped things up, I slowed things down," he said. "I built assignments for people to go at their own pace, then assignments to keep everyone together. I put absolutely every note and problem in a packet and handed it to them so that they really didn't need to show up, and then I tried handing out nothing at all so that everything had to be written down in class."

Michael read one book that claimed the only thing that mattered to students was that you were concerned about them. So then he went to great lengths to engage students in conversations about themselves. One student that term wrote in a review that "it's like he's pretending to be our friend because he's not a very good teacher." Which, in truth, was exactly what he was doing.

"I was like a dog chasing its tail. I was going after something I could not get no matter how fast I went or how hard I tried," Michael said.

Michael had run out of new things to try when a chance conversation with a former student turned him around. "She said to me, as delicately as possible, 'Why are you still a bad teacher when you could be a great something else?'

"And I had no answer," Michael said. "I had looked at my failures in teaching from so many different angles, but not from the most basic, the most obvious, one. Maybe I'm just not meant for that kind of work."

The wheels started spinning in Michael's mind. He had

always wanted to be a paramedic. No, that would be crazy, he thought. Then again, maybe he could still be a paramedic. Granted, he would be the rare paramedic with an advanced mathematics degree, but surely he could work around that.

Five years into the job now, Michael still feels the charge of adrenaline every time he steps into the ambulance to begin his shift. "Nobody cares if the paramedic isn't interesting when he comes to save you," he said. "In fact, in this job, boring is a comfort to people."

"I WILL NEVER forget the feeling the first time they had us all line up in school to measure our height and weight," Tess said. "Our teacher stood next to an old-fashioned scale, the kind where you have to nudge the little weighted box over the numbers and try to get the bar to stay straight between the lines. And she just kept nudging and nudging and nudging. And everyone in class could see that box had to be moved way over to the edge when she stopped to write down my numbers."

Tess vowed that day to lose enough weight so that the next time they measured the class, no one would stare at the scale.

Forty-some years later, Tess was still fighting against her weight, trying all kinds of diets and obsessing about everything she ate. Like Michael's struggle against failing in his job, Tess would learn the hard way that no amount of effort can fix a problem that you put at the center of your life.

"'Try harder,' that's what we all learn we're supposed to do when we're facing a big problem," Tess said. But the harder she tried, the worse it was. Because when she kept her focus on food all day long she lost twice over—first, she was miserable every minute of the day trying to avoid every extra calorie, and second, in the end she would give in anyway and feel awful about that.

Just as she had as a child, Tess felt very alone in her struggle. As far as she knew, no one in her family or among her coworkers and friends had ever tried to lose more than a few pounds, and none had been trying all their lives.

When she saw an ad from a local university seeking volunteers for a research study on eating habits, Tess didn't think she would find any answers, but she thought that she might at least meet some people who understood what she had been going through.

At an orientation session, Tess learned that the study she had joined was investigating people eating too much of the wrong foods. "They could do that entire study just on me," Tess joked. "I said that to the woman seated next to me, who just gave me a nod like she felt exactly the same way."

The researchers had Tess and the others try out different ways to avoid their favorite junk foods. Some made a list of what foods they would avoid; others had to come up with plans to avoid situations where junk foods would be available or create a list of rules about what and when they could eat.

Months later Tess learned the outcome of the study. It turned out that no matter which rules or lists or plans people made, they didn't eat less junk food, *they ate more*.

The effect was ironic, but the logic simple. People in the study spent all day thinking about what they were trying to avoid, until the effort to deny themselves defeated them. Like somebody trying to follow the instruction "don't think about an elephant," they were up against the impossibility of constantly thinking about not thinking about something.

When the researchers explained what they had found, Tess was elated. "It was like that instant when light finally peeks over the horizon in the morning," she said. *"The problem is the problem.* I understood it immediately because that's exactly how I have lived my life: try harder, do worse."

Counselors from the university offered help to study participants who sought it. For Tess, the study and the counseling turned her approach to eating and her weight upside down. "'Can't' and 'don't' and words like that went out of my life," she said. "Instead they helped me deal with food more like I deal with the rest of my life. I don't spend all day long thinking about a manicure, I get one once in a while and I enjoy it, but then I go right along with regular life. And now I am that way with what I eat. I eat real food every day, and I eat a junk food as a treat once in a while."

Slowly, but surely, Tess has lost some weight since the study ended. "More importantly, the cake and pastries monster isn't in control of my life anymore," Tess said. "Now I'm in control."

As a schoolboy, Philip Schultz suffered through an almost unbearable routine centered on the problem that defined his life. As Ben Curtis and Michael and Tess's experience showed, as Jannson and Smith's research shows, putting a problem first each day means waging a constantly losing battle. For Philip Schultz, like the others, progress could not begin until he put the problem aside.

Each day, Philip's teacher would begin a new lesson and he would be at full attention, sitting straight in his desk, pencil in hand. Each day he would try to do the work. And each day he would fail. Again and again he watched his classmates learn new things while he sat painfully stymied, hoping not to be noticed.

His teachers knew not to call on him because he never had the right answer. Over time, they would lose any faith that they could do anything to reach him, so they moved him to the back of the room and gradually shut him out of their lessons and their thoughts. His classmates, however, never lost interest in the slow boy they took such delight in tormenting.

School administrators finally took notice of Philip after he lashed out at some of the boys who had teased him. The principal solved the problem by asking Philip's parents to find him another school. Not surprisingly, repeating the third grade in a new school was a joyless process that served only to bring Philip the same frustrations and failures he had experienced the first time.

The source of all his difficulties was simple, but especially cruel for a young boy who grew up in a house full of books: Philip could not read. His parents, his teachers, and various tutors had worked with him for years without making headway. Far from actually reading, for Philip it was a losing battle merely to get letters to stand their ground on the page. Though at the time he had never heard the word, Philip was profoundly dyslexic.

One tutor saw Philip's inability to read as evidence of laziness. He snidely asked Philip, "What are you going to be in life if you can't read?" Philip gave the only answer he could think of: "I'll be a writer." The tutor laughed, an enormous laugh that shook his whole body.

Not being able to read was the central fact of Philip's life. His failures mounted on top of other failures. And he came to believe, in his heart, that he was stupid.

Convinced that the stupid boy he had turned out to be would never learn to read, would never succeed, Philip gave up on himself. *But* he did not give up on the pretend version of himself that he kept in his head.

In his head, imaginary Philip would go on to be a writer. Imaginary Philip would succeed in school. Imaginary Philip would get his letters to stand their ground because imaginary Philip knew how to read.

While his real life was defined by an insurmountable problem, imaginary Philip's life was defined by possibility and promise.

Hidden away in his room, freed from the burden of his limitations, Philip put this new version of himself to work, slowly making headway associating words with the sounds he had heard his mother read aloud to him.

And in the process of creating a character with the traits he most wanted to have, and turning himself into that character, real Philip taught himself to read. And true to his promise, he found joy in his love for words and the music of language. Despite his tutor's cackles, Philip Schultz grew up to become an internationally decorated poet.

It is telling, for someone who turned his source of childhood misery into his life's work, that Schultz is most famous for a Pulitzer Prize–winning collection of poems entitled *Failure*. Nonetheless, looking back at his experience decades later, Philip focuses not on the pain of his condition but on the power of creating a way through it. "I had to stop seeing what everyone else saw when they looked at me. I had to stop seeing my flaws first," he said. "When I did that, I was free."

THE TAKEAWAY

Constantly thinking about his problem stopped young Philip Schultz on page one. It knocked Ben Curtis off the PGA Tour. It left Michael making himself dizzy squeezing a square peg into a round job. It led Tess to do exactly what she was trying to avoid.

Thinking about problems first limits what we can accomplish in real, tangible ways.

Thinking about problems first makes us seventeen times more likely to fail.[2]

Imagine you are at the circus right now.

Your problems are in the center ring—they are the lion tamer and the trapeze artists. You can't take your eyes or your thoughts off them; nor do you even try, because your problems are fascinating and important. But they are also discouraging and intimidating, and draining.

Your solutions—transformative ideas that would enrich your life: They are a guy with popcorn, walking slowly up an aisle, clear on the other side of the giant tent. You can see him and even study him if you care to, but the odds are you will never notice him because he's not where you've trained your mind to look. And even if you glance toward him, you won't pay him any attention. But he's right there, and he has what you need.

Two for the Road: Two Ways to Put Your Problem Down Right Now

Go watch a boring movie. François Jacob won a Nobel Prize for work that revealed how genes make life possible. The central insight of his life's work didn't come to him during the countless hours he spent in the laboratory. It came to him at the movies—more specifically, a "dull" movie that left his mind free to wander about. When you are stuck, find a good distraction that takes you away from your problems and sets your mind free.

– – – – – – – –

Be someone else for a while. Looking at a problem the same way over and over again is entirely unproductive. We will fail unless we give our minds a way to look at the situation from a new perspective. Psychologists Darya Zabelina and Michael Robinson found that simply asking their adult study participants to imagine themselves as seven-year-olds vastly increased their creative output on a variety of challenging tasks.[3] You will need to see the same things differently to come up with new ideas, so look at those things the way someone else would.

CHAPTER 2

Humans, Swamp People, and the Survival Problem

WHAT IF YOU could spend the next six months studying happiness and joy or the next six months studying unhappiness and pain?

It's a tiny test, but within it lies a measure of our fundamental orientation in everything we do. Are we drawn to good or bad? Do we think more about what we want or what we want to avoid? Do we begin by looking for a solution or a problem?

On the surface this seems like an easy question. Surely the happiness study would be a lot more fun, and the results would be just as useful—if not more useful, since no one is going to want to imitate the behavior of the unhappy.

We know how psychologists have answered this question in real life. A researcher built a database of tens of thousands of psychological studies, separating out the work that was looking for what's right with people from the work that was looking for what's wrong. It turns out that psychologists were producing

125 percent more research studies on unhappiness and problems than happiness and solutions.[1]

The source of our problem-first, bad-news bias is as simple and as old as time. It was fundamental to the caveman 400,000 years ago and to the psychology professor doing research last semester, and is fundamental to everyone you know today. We link an understanding of negative outcomes and danger to our very survival. We are driven to pay attention to what's wrong professionally, personally, and in everything we care about, from bad weather to the last-second shot that costs our favorite team the game.

At one time this all made sense. If you were focused on the good things in life and ignored the threats, a saber-toothed tiger could eat you for lunch while you were making a list of reasons to be happy. Today, however, this orientation toward danger and fear and problems and negativity stifles our creativity, our ability to find solutions, and ultimately our lives—all in the service of avoiding being eaten by a saber-toothed tiger that went extinct 12,000 years ago. We have let this asymmetry between bad and good persist as an act of self-protection, but now paying attention to danger is a bigger threat to our lives than the danger itself.

AT ITS PEAK in the late 1990s, *Seinfeld* was making the NBC television network $200 million in annual profits. In fact, the network was making more money from *Seinfeld* than from all its other prime-time shows combined. The show was a critical and popular success, holding a unique position as a dominant and dependable force in the ratings, week after week drawing upwards of 20 million viewers and ultimately being named the greatest television series of all time by *TV Guide*. Years later, key lines from the show still reverberate in popular culture (not that there's anything wrong with that), and the show remains a mainstay in syndication.

To this day, both star and cocreator Jerry Seinfeld and NBC programming chief Warren Littlefield, who ultimately put the show on the air, keep framed copies by their desks of the very same piece of *Seinfeld* memorabilia. While for Jerry Seinfeld it's a lesson in irony, and for Littlefield it's a lesson in decision making, both have preserved copies of the test audience report measuring reactions to *Seinfeld*'s pilot episode.

The pilot episode is made for that purpose. An entire, full-scale episode is created to let network executives study whether they think audiences will like the show. Based on the pilot, networks place orders for a full or partial season's worth of episodes, or they shelve the project completely.

What did the test audience say about *Seinfeld*? They hated it. They didn't like the characters, the style, the setting, or the story. George was a "loser" and a "wimp." Jerry's life was "boring." And the Kramer character (then called Kessler) didn't make sense. Only Elaine escaped the test audience's derision—because her character hadn't been created yet. Even the format of the show, featuring short bits of stand-up comedy before and after the story line, bothered the test audience.

Jerry Seinfeld himself derisively describes the test report as demonstrating that the show "didn't appeal to every genus, from humans to swamp people." But the report suggested something far worse to the network: The show didn't appeal to anyone. Brandon Tartikoff, Littlefield's boss at NBC, read the report and understood immediately that the audience thought *Seinfeld* was "too Jewish, too New York."

Littlefield called the test results "weak" and "disastrous." He thought Seinfeld the person was very funny. He thought *Seinfeld* the show had enormous potential. But the audience report loomed. "It *scared* us," he said.

And that fear was all-encompassing. "There is a bottom line here," Littlefield said. "We have to think about that. I have to answer for that bottom line. And if I go out on a limb for a show the research says will falter, how do I account for myself?"

Littlefield saw the choice he had to make on *Seinfeld* as a dangerous problem. If he passed, he was throwing away talent and potential. On the other hand, if he spent good money on a bad show, a show he knew was different from the usual fare and that test audiences were resistant to, he would take the blame. It would be very hard to walk into a boardroom and explain why he made a show based on characters, stories, and a format nobody liked.

Littlefield and his team passed on *Seinfeld*. Instead, they gave the green light to *Sister Kate*. "We went with things that had better testing. We chose a nun who took care of orphans over *Seinfeld*," Littlefield admits.

Network enthusiasm for *Sister Kate* and her adorable orphans was such that they ordered a full season of episodes. The sister and her wards were relatable, wholesome, warm. And they were canceled before the first season even ended because the show was painfully mediocre. (Here's an actual joke from *Sister Kate*, in which Sister Kate describes her friend, April, who drives slowly: "When the speed limit's twenty-five, she goes twenty-four!")

While *Sister Kate* could not be less threatening or disruptive, the *Seinfeld* world was full of anger and petty annoyance, desperation and frustration, and just plain weirdness. While Seinfeld once described *Seinfeld* as the show with no hugging, *Sister Kate* was the very embodiment of the show that hugs its audience.

"You step back from the situation, and it would be hard to imagine *Sister Kate* really working. I mean, could this even conceivably be a hit," Littlefield admits. "But back up to when you are in that moment, and you have a stack of glowing words about one show, and basically loathing for the other, which would you choose?"

That is the lure of the problem. It feels safer. It's easier to explain. But it closes our minds off to possibilities.

The *Seinfeld* pilot would ultimately turn up on NBC, not because executives had changed their mind but because they were out of new material from their network shows and traditionally "burned off" dead pilots in otherwise empty summer time slots. Not surprisingly, the single episode of an unknown new show airing without promotion on a random summer night did not attract a big audience.

But the show did gain one fan in Rick Ludwin, the NBC executive in charge of late-night programming and specials. Ludwin saw something in *Seinfeld* that he didn't see anywhere else on prime-time television: original humor, not a minor variation on an old formula. Though they had never done anything like this before, Ludwin offered to pay for four additional episodes of *Seinfeld* out of his late-night budget. With that sliver of an opening, first four episodes, then a half-season, then a full season of the show were ordered, and the show nobody liked became the top-rated comedy on television.

With twenty years to think about how he almost missed airing the greatest moneymaker of his career, Littlefield points to the power of fear. Audience research, he says now, is always going to spit out its first taste of any show that isn't "easily digestible" or "that tries to be extraordinary and different." But it's that extraordinary quality that can draw viewers in and hold on to them. It's that extraordinary quality that he was in business to find.

Littlefield looks at the *Seinfeld* research report now and smiles. "It says why no one likes these characters and why the show will never work." From the biggest mistake he nearly made, he's learned that you must disregard warnings that leave you incapable of acting. "Forget the research," he says now. "It's about a vision."

The lesson has hardly been absorbed across the industry. Jeff Zucker, who later ran NBC for a decade, warns that *Seinfeld* would not be possible today on network television. Even if it survived the pilot test debacle, it would not have been given a chance to build an audience. "If it wasn't a hit immediately, it would be gone," Zucker said. Why? "No one would have the guts to let it find its way."

THE FIRST NIGHT was a celebration of fate. Gina and Kevin had both logged in on the same Thursday evening to play Words with Friends, an online word game similar to Scrabble. Contrary to the name of the game, neither sought out a friend to play against, instead opting for a random opponent. They could be matched up against anyone from anywhere. But the game matched them against each other.

Soon the chat box filled as the two playfully mixed compli-
ments and gentle taunts, dropping word after word into place.
After Gina won big by using all seven letters to make the word
elation, they both kept hitting the rematch button, and in short
order, game one gave way to game two, game three, and game
four. By the end of the night, they had made a virtual date to
play again. They played and chatted again, moving from conversation about the game to swapping stories about their work
and their lives. By the end of the weekend, when they finally
got around to discussing where they lived, they were shocked to
find out that in a game with an international following, they
were only two hundred miles away from each other. Elation was
the word on both their minds.

Unlike the research reports on *Seinfeld,* all indicators were
positive. It was easy to move forward.

Three weeks later they met for dinner. It was awkward at
first. They were two people who felt connected, yet they were
meeting for the first time. They weren't sure whether this was
dinner with a friend or dinner with a stranger. They stumbled a bit looking for conversation, feeling the pressure to fill
the spaces that did not seem to exist when the game, the
computer, and two hundred miles were between them.
Searching for that feeling, that chemistry they had felt before, Kevin half-seriously suggested they fire up Words with
Friends and pretend they weren't sitting three feet away from
each other.

Heading back home, Kevin thought that Gina was nice
enough but that their real-life selves were just not as well matched
as their virtual selves. Gina, on the other hand, saw things quite
differently. Kevin arrived home to find several emails from

Gina, including one with the subject line "Gina's list of dinner highlights," another with a recap of the best words each had played during their old Words matches, and a third declaring that they shared something special.

Kevin was surprised to see that Gina's perception of the evening, and of everything, was so different from his, and that she had put so much thought into cataloguing every moment they had shared. Kevin was even more convinced, since they saw things so differently, that there really was no future here for the two of them.

Gina did not take the rejection well. After several pleas to change Kevin's mind, she began a series of unwelcome intrusions into Kevin's life. She left emails, voicemails, and text messages. She showed up on his doorstep late one night. Gina followed Kevin to a bar where he was meeting friends. Her pleas for a second chance gave way to her issuing vague warnings.

Kevin was petrified. Gina was obviously unbalanced, but would this lead to something worse? Would he come out of his house one day to see the tires on his car slashed? Was she capable of some kind of violence?

By the time Kevin went to court seeking a restraining order, his evidence of harassment included not only voicemails, emails, and texts but a cell phone video recording Kevin made of Gina shouting obscenities at him from the sidewalk in front of his place.

Ultimately, even though the trip to court seemed to snap Gina out of her delusional behavior, the worst effects of the stalking were yet to come.

Kevin found himself a changed person. Once the picture

of calm, now he was jittery and nervous. Once confident and warm, now he was distant. "I always feel like someone is watching me. I'm always looking over my shoulder," Kevin said.

"In a normal life, I never thought about what always being afraid does to a person," Kevin said. "Almost everything I did, I took for granted. I could do things without a second thought. But when you're afraid, that's the only thing that comes easy. It's the only thing. Everything else is a struggle."

When Kevin met someone a year later, the relationship held all the promise in the world. Kevin thought this might be the one. They moved in together, and Kevin began thinking that marriage was imminent.

But he had grown accustomed to being on edge, constantly ready to argue and fall into a rage. Kevin saw himself poisoning a relationship he should have treasured. Even waking up in his girlfriend's arms could induce a brief panic as he momentarily imagined that the person lying next to him must have broken into his home.

"If the point of all this was to make me miserable, it worked better than Gina could have imagined," Kevin said. "Because she infected every single aspect of my life. In the space of a few months, I lost my relationship, I moved, I lost my peace of mind. I even lost my sense of who I was. That was all cast away in fear and loathing."

Kevin acted out of a basic survival instinct. He took by far the biggest problem he was facing and gave it sustained attention. And in the process he made it worse. He enlarged the problem. He fed the problem by giving it an active place in his life at a point when it could have been reduced to a bad memory. It started with a self-protective impulse, but it ended with a diminished quality of life.

"You have to start to live again," Kevin tells himself now.

You have just won the lottery. The biggest check you've ever seen has just come, and it's safely in your bank account. It's the kind of sudden good fortune that people dream about and wish for all their lives.

How happy are you now? Have you ever been happier? Is every part of your life better now? Are your burdens fading away?

We know the answer to these questions, because Philip Brinkman went out and tracked down lottery winners and asked them about their general happiness and their daily joys and frustrations.

For comparison's sake, he asked the same questions to a second group of people, whose lives were otherwise very similar—except for one thing: Like most people, they had never won the lottery.

Which group do you think is happier, lottery winners or regular people? The answer seems obvious.

But the obvious answer is wrong. Good fortune can be worse than no fortune, as the *lottery winners took 10 percent less pleasure from daily life events than ordinary people.*[2] Even when they were asked how happy they imagined themselves to be in the future, the lottery winners were not more optimistic than ordinary people.

Lottery winners are basically ordinary people with an extra million dollars in their pockets. How can they be no happier than the next person? How can they be less happy? This makes no sense.

But that is how we are wired. Good things, ultimately, are secondary to bad things. Good breaks down over time. We get used to good things, and it raises our expectations. If you spend your lottery winnings on a giant house, at some point it stops being a shockingly large and nice house, and it just becomes your house. And good makes other things seem boring. After you win the lottery, how excited will you be about reading an interesting magazine article or buying a nice pair of pants? Good fades.

Bad things, on the other hand, are always compelling to us. Bad is so compelling to us that even when we have every incentive to value good over bad, we value bad over good.

You are married and you have just agreed to answer some questions about your life and relationship. Really basic stuff. But you and your spouse have to be there at the same time for the interview.

They bring you two into a small room. You sit side by side behind a table, with a researcher on the other side. There's a two-way mirror behind the researcher. Presumably someone on the other side is taking notes.

The questions are easy. Maybe a bit nosy, but nothing outlandish. Where did you two meet? Who takes out the garbage? How do you like to spend your free time? And so forth.

The researcher wants to hear from both of you, so it can take a while to finish off even a simple question.

Do you smile at your spouse? Do you listen closely? Do you nod? Do you touch your spouse on the hand or shoulder at some point during the interview?

Do you interrupt your spouse to add or correct something? Do you roll your eyes at a criticism or an embarrassing answer? Do you shift uncomfortably in your seat when your spouse goes on talking?

The researchers did not actually care where you met or who puts the trash out. They wanted to know if you were more likely to mimic the friendly behaviors or the unfriendly behaviors of your spouse.

Though everything would be easier in life if you repeated the good more than the bad, in fact we are five times more likely to repeat the unfriendly gestures.[3] That means that for every single thing you are doing wrong, you'd better be doing five things right or you are going backwards.

Research also shows that our tendency to focus on what's wrong is not only out of date as a survival instinct, it has actually become an active burden to the species. For survival purposes, a healthy, fulfilling sex life should produce a thriving relationship, and therefore maximize the likelihood of reproduction. But when a couple's sex life is good, research shows that accounts for only 20 percent of their relationship satisfaction. When a couple's sex life is unfulfilling, however, that fact accounts for 75 percent of their relationship dissatisfaction. In other words, good sex doesn't keep us together, but bad sex drives us apart.[4]

Negative things mattered more than positive, fear ruled the day, and problems defined life for lottery winners and married couples, for Kevin and for NBC. The primal fear inclination to see bad over good is, at this point, a survival instinct that has survived too long. Letting our natural impulses rule keeps us fearful and down all day long. It would all be more than enough to keep the caveman inside all day. But we have to get out of the cave.

GOING OUT, HOWEVER, is exactly what proved to be increasingly difficult and frustrating for Claire.

"It sounds ridiculous, I know," Claire acknowledges. "How can you be reluctant to go out the door after heading out that very same door every day for forty years? But it's different when you don't have any place to go."

Rising from the mailroom to office manager to branch manager to a place on the senior management team at corporate headquarters, Claire had been in the banking industry since the days of passbook accounts and free toasters. She considers herself very fortunate that her entire career provided work she found challenging and useful. "You go around town, and you can't help but see it," Claire said. "Everywhere you go you see a business built on a loan from my bank, you see a family moving into a house bought with a mortgage from us, you see customers who lived their lives around the savings they kept with us week after week, year after year."

Day-to-day in the office, Claire was always a decision maker. "Even when I was just starting out, within weeks I was reorganizing how we filed everything," she said. "And by the end, I was making decisions that had seven- and eight-figure implications before I had even finished my first cup of coffee."

Now, her agenda is less compelling.

"I get dressed. I eat breakfast. I seem to be in a hurry to get ready. But for what?" she said. "I'm rushing to go nowhere."

Making matters worse is the fact that Claire recognizes she

is battling against something she should treasure. "What is time? Time is the greatest asset you could possibly have. Even the pharaohs ran out of time. And what I am doing with the greatest asset I could ever have?" she asked. "I've turned it into nothing. Worse than nothing. It's become a threat I have to try to manage, to tame, try to keep it from destroying me. That's funny, isn't it, trying to keep existence from destroying me."

Retirement was once a prospect she had welcomed. On the horizon, it seemed like a series of possibilities. Now that she is actually retired, though, she has trouble recalling what any of them were. Everyone in her life tells her she's free, while she feels trapped. "Free to do precisely what?" she wonders. "Because I don't have the slightest idea."

She looked into joining various groups, but if the crowd was too young she felt like she was the old lady ruining the fun. And if the crowd was too old, she felt like *just another* old lady lost among all that white hair.

"I just have this recurring feeling that I'm showing up to a party I wasn't invited to," Claire said. She yearns for the familiar, for something that feels comfortable to her. "The only thing I can think of is going back to the bank, but I just left there."

Though she didn't have a tangible fear like Kevin or the NBC executives, Claire's problem was just as central a feature of her life. Indeed, once she converted her retirement into a problem, she couldn't see any way out of it.

"People say, 'You have the time to do anything, try something new.' But do you remember that first day of kindergarten feeling? That was sixty years ago for me. I remember it, and it was petrifying. I could either go through that or stay home. So I stay home."

In any walk of life, having the guts to get past negative reactions, to get past bad news, to get past fear—it opens up a world of possibilities. Indeed, overcoming fear makes it possible to redefine a problem, or even the entire universe.

THE IMAGE OF Albert Einstein, the most respected physicist in the world, sticking out his tongue like a naughty four-year-old remains striking even now, nearly seven decades after the picture was taken. How can we reconcile our thoughts about a man in possession of such a great mind and such juvenile inclinations? But that is the wrong question. Flip the question on its head and suddenly the frivolous behavior seems invaluable. After all, are there any great thinkers without some unusual tendencies? Are there any great minds timidly set for conformity?

Though silly and trivial on the surface, the Einstein photo reveals something essential about big ideas and the people who create them. Do you know what Einstein did when he saw that photo for the first time? He didn't wince or turn away. He didn't issue a public apology or vow to be more mature. He asked for a copy of the photo. Then he had it cropped so that the focus was entirely on his face—and tongue. And then he had copies printed up as note cards so that when he was moved to jot a note to one of his very learned and dignified colleagues, the person first had to look at Einstein sticking out his tongue.

When Einstein won the Nobel Prize, it was less his speech accepting the award than what he did afterward that illustrates the nature of his ability to cast aside what others assume and see things anew. From Stockholm, Einstein left to visit with his friend Niels Bohr, the noted physicist, in Copenhagen. Bohr met Einstein at the Copenhagen train station and led him to a streetcar that would take them close to Bohr's home.

They took a seat on the streetcar and quickly fell into deep conversation about their favorite subject, quantum mechanics. By the time Bohr thought to look up, they were at the end of the line, having long since missed their stop. Sheepishly, Bohr led them back onto the streetcar now heading the other way. Resolving to actually get off at the right stop, Bohr nevertheless became so engrossed in discussion with Einstein that when he looked up again they were back where they had started, pulling into the Copenhagen train station. As he led his friend onto the streetcar for a third attempt to go home, Bohr felt ridiculous. "I can well imagine what people were thinking," Bohr said, assuming that the motorman must have believed that these two men riding back and forth on the streetcar were not right in the head. What was also obvious to Bohr was that it never occurred to Einstein to think, much less worry, that others might see them as odd. Whether it was his theories or even his methods of riding public transportation, Einstein didn't seek anyone's approval.

In those tiny moments of Einstein's life, the essence of his strength was on display. His superpower, as it were, was a willingness to exist inside his own world, losing not a moment trapped inside the fear problem. He could have absolutely fearless thoughts. He could venture down a path no one had ever trod. And he could do it without hesitation because he wasn't ducking danger and he wasn't worried about consequences.

Indeed, Einstein saw his own strengths in similar terms. "I am a horse for single harness, not cut out for tandem or team work," he wrote. Most people, he understood, would have trouble living outside the limits placed by the judgment of others. It takes strength and sometimes requires a willingness to stand well apart from your peers. But by incurring the cost of this distance, Einstein said, "I am compensated for it by being rendered independent of the customs, opinions, and prejudices of others and am not tempted to rest my peace of mind upon such shifting foundations."

While finding his independence invaluable to his work, Einstein hardly held himself above others. Instead, he argued that we all underestimate our capabilities because we tend to look at ourselves from the wrong angle. "Everyone is a genius," Einstein said. "But if you judge a fish on its ability to climb a tree, it will live its whole life believing that it is stupid."

THE TAKEAWAY

Fear of the problem knocked Kevin out of his heart and home and kept Claire locked in hers. Fear put *Seinfeld* on the shelf while NBC invested in the utterly forgettable *Sister Kate*. And it was the extraordinary absence of the fear impulse that helped make Albert Einstein's career possible.

Fear of the problem is there. It's in us all. And where it once kept us from an early death at the hands of predators, today it keeps us from living a full life by putting our biggest problems in the center of our field of vision. **It is fear of the problem that makes the bad in our relationships five times more influential than the good.** It is primal fear that makes psychologists, who should really know better, who should be able to overcome anachronistic, instinctive tendencies, put twice as much effort into studying what's wrong with us over what's right.

Letting fear guide our lives, letting fear put our problems first, is a lot like refusing to climb past the first rung of a ladder when you're painting a two-story house. It's safer that way, sure, but only if you don't actually want to accomplish anything.

TWO FOR THE ROAD: TWO STEPS AWAY
FROM THE FEAR PROBLEM

Do something you've never done before. What did Neil Young do after he released his first Number 1 hit song "Heart of Gold"? Instead of worrying if he could do it all over again, he went in an entirely new musical direction. "This song put me in the middle of the road," he said. "Traveling there soon became a bore so I headed for the ditch. A rougher ride but I saw more interesting people there." In the process, he sustained a career that has spanned more than four decades. There is such great freedom of thought when you do not limit yourself to what you already know and what you've already done. Do something today—anything— that is totally unfamiliar to you.

- - - - - - - -

Eat a candy bar. Instead of fear, we actually think more clearly when we feel a little bit of joy. How easy is that to access? It's as simple as a piece of candy. Alice Isen and her colleagues did an experiment with medical doctors.[5] Half received a small bag of candy filled with miniature Hershey's chocolate bars. Half did not. She gave all the doctors the same patient file and asked them to offer a diagnosis. The candy eaters were vastly more likely to arrive at the correct diagnosis (chronic active hepatitis), and they also performed better on a test of creativity. Even the tiniest source of joy today will spur you to better ideas.

CHAPTER 3

Power and the Farb Problem

WHAT IF YOU were in charge for a day?

You're the president, the pope, or the CEO of a giant company. What are you going to do?

You will search for problems. You will search for problems because it is in problems that you will make yourself consequential. It's all well and good to be in charge, but if you don't find any problems, what difference did you make?

Though it sounds like the premise of a reality TV show, legend has it that Saul Wahl was literally king for a day in Poland in 1587. And in that day he identified twenty-six problems and issued more than sixty orders.

Problems may well stop us in our tracks, seeking problems may well start with our primal fear impulses, but problems are also a great source of urgency. A problem is all alarms and action and consequence. A problem is a very seductive thing. And its hold over us is universal. It is not just kings and kings for a day, it's in all of us, all the time. Everyone feels more important when pointing out problems.

We insert ourselves into problems like police officers giving tickets. Problems make us feel necessary. They make us feel powerful. They make us feel alive. If we don't have a problem, we have a problem.

AMID THE MANY treasures that have made their way to the Rock and Roll Hall of Fame from world-famous stages and recording studios sits a weathered piece of paper. There are no lyrics, no melodies, no grand plans for an album or a concert scratched out on it. But the document offers just the barest hint of a revolution that would arrive a decade later and change not only music but pretty much everything. Succinct and precise, John Lennon's high school report card suggests a rather underwhelming student who never seemed to come up with quite the right answer because he was too busy looking at things differently than everybody else.

Under his mediocre grades, one teacher at the Quarry Bank school wrote in the space for comments that Lennon had achieved "a poor result due to the fact that he spends most of his time devising 'witty' remarks." Lest his meaning be misconstrued, he actually put witty in quotation marks. That is, not only did Lennon waste his time on humor, but he didn't even have a proper boy's wit. Certainly he said nothing that his teachers considered amusing or interesting. If only he could put aside his pointless wordplay and frivolity, his teachers thought, maybe he would amount to something.

The juxtaposition of this report of a failure preserved forever in a house of triumph tells us something important about our passion for problems. John Lennon's teachers had been trained to offer conventional lessons and make conventional measurements in the service of producing conventional success. They believed that stepping outside that process was surely a path to failure, and they were on vigilant watch for the first signs that someone was heading in that direction.

To root out this problem, Lennon was favored with constant discipline. Day after day he was kept for detention. There he sat, crouched over his papers, writing "I must not . . ." over and over again, before filling in the precise nature of his latest offense. Other days Lennon was made to do chores around the school building. And when the standard punishments had no effect, Lennon was summoned to the headmaster's office for a caning.

School officials saw the problem very clearly, and they were absolutely certain of the consequences. Lennon had begun Quarry Bank in the A cluster, a group of students offered the most challenging courses and expected to enroll at fine universities. By his second year, he had been downgraded to the B cluster. By the end of his fourth year, he was exiled to the C cluster, of whom very little was expected. By the time he reached the Cs, his report cards no longer offered gentle chiding but spelled out the situation in stark terms. "Certainly on the road to failure," one year-end report noted. He is, in a word, "Hopeless." To the headmaster, the evidence was clear and convincing: This boy had no future.

Later, the staff took some satisfaction in Lennon's performance on the comprehensive exams given to college-bound British students. Lennon failed nine out of nine tests—just as they had warned he would.

No one appreciated the remarkable thoughts and utterly

original perspectives their most vexing student was capable of producing. Nor did his teachers—who wore imposing black gowns and lorded over a student body itself decked out in matching black blazers, each bearing the school's awkward Latin motto (*Ex Hoc Metallo Virtutem* . . . From This Rough Metal We Forge Virtue)—ever notice what their student was teaching himself when they weren't looking.

Out of their sight, John Lennon was a bookworm, reading, writing, drawing, thinking. He created his own journal, the *Daily Howl*, filled with his own stories, poems, and cartoons. He began devouring a twenty-volume set of the world's great short stories as a ten-year old. He was, ironically, a model student when he wasn't in a classroom.

But a piece of metal to be forged he was not. He hated regimentation, being told what to do, or when to do it. He hated having to fit within the stifling standards and judgments of the Quarry Bank staff. And so he didn't.

To be sure, it wasn't just school officials who marked Lennon as a disruptive and aimless force. Everyone saw that. "I was the one who all the other boys' parents—including Paul's father—would say, 'Keep away from him,'" Lennon later recounted. Imagine if Paul McCartney's father had been successful in that effort.

Even at home, the aunt who raised him would periodically blow through his room to collect his various stacks of writing and toss them in the garbage lest they clutter the place. In high school, as his devotion to music bloomed, she famously warned him, "The guitar's all very well, John, but you'll never make a living at it."

The problem was obvious to everyone. This boy wasn't doing what you're supposed to do. This problem, like all problems, demanded a response. We will push and shove and try with all our might to move problems out of our way. And we will enjoy the exertion because it is pleasing to be right. It is pleasing to know what to do.

Promise and potential and answers, on the other hand, are hard to see. We may have never quite seen it before. We may not recognize it. And even if we did, what do we do with it? How would we nurture it? To admit that Lennon was bright and full of promise, his teachers would have had to surrender to uncertainty and risk their own irrelevance. To admit that Lennon was bright and full of promise they would have had to acknowledge that there might be more he could teach them than they could teach him. Instead, Lennon's teachers labeled a problem the most extraordinary student they would ever know.

Happily, Lennon never believed the consensus opinion of him. "When I was about 12 I used to think I must be a genius, but nobody's noticed," he said looking back on his school years.

A decade removed from Quarry Bank, Lennon heard from his old school again. A student there wrote him a letter. He said they studied his lyrics in English class to decipher their meaning. Could Lennon be of any help in that regard, the student wondered? Lennon found the idea hilarious. Even then, his old teachers were still trying to make sense of him, still trying to impose their standards on his writings, still trying to make him fit into something they understood. In their honor, Lennon wrote the song "I Am the Walrus," with the sole intention of confounding anyone's efforts to make sense of the words.

IT WASN'T THE time she was the only person who was annoyed that the office Christmas lunch had leaked past its allotted time and was still going strong into its third hour of the workday. It wasn't the time she found herself pulling the curtains closed tight against the sunshine, the view, and the ocean breeze to cut down on the glare as she checked her work messages on her phone during her first vacation in two years. And it wasn't the time she stepped out into the lobby during the intermission of a touring Broadway musical, only to lose track of time while flipping through messages and to be told the second act had already started and she could not return to her seat in the second row of the theater.

None of these experiences made Linda think that she was way too plugged into the office and that she needed to reexamine her approach to work.

But when she found herself sneaking out of her mother's hospital room and darting down the hallway to find a quiet place to take a work call, Linda began to suspect she had taken things too far.

Linda doesn't blame her boss. Or her coworkers. It wasn't a bad culture that turned her into some kind of always-on office robot. This was a trap she built herself. "It was just me," she said. "It was who I was, what I needed, or thought I needed.

"I believed the way you proved your value was to be there, be ready to go," she added. "When you work in the commodities business, you have to realize that everything can change, not just overnight, but in a moment. I thought, How can I afford to cut myself off for a week at a time on vacation, or even for a lunch hour, for that matter?"

Like John Lennon's teachers, Linda wanted desperately to matter. If there was a meeting, she wanted to be at it. If there was a memo, she wanted to read it first. If there was anything happening anywhere, she wanted to know it. "The nightmare image for me is to be on the wrong side of a closed door," Linda said. "I want to be on the side where big things happen, not on the side that watches and waits."

Not surprisingly, what developed was not just an enormous strain on all her time—at work, after work, on the way to work, on vacation—but a never-ending source of stress. "When you put yourself on call like that, every little message is a new emergency. You get the message, and you pounce on it, and you fix the problem," Linda said. To keep track of everything coming and going out, Linda moved every message out of her email inbox the moment she addressed it. She didn't leave the office if there was a still a message waiting for her. And she didn't go to bed until the box was empty again each night.

Ironically, even when Linda didn't get a message, it became stressful to her. "You think, Why aren't there any messages? Is the system down? Is the problem so big there's not even time to send out a message?

"It's ridiculous, but it seems sort of reasonable to you when you're doing it."

Living every moment of every day as a problem left Linda exhausted but unable to sleep restfully even when her head hit the pillow. Of course, she had trained her body not for deep rest but for constant alert.

With all her dedication and zeal, Linda had left herself no real time to stop, to digest, to think. Which meant that there was never any time for anything different, or better. She couldn't give the company a new idea or a better way to do things because she was too busy to ever think of one. Like a car up on blocks, she was spinning her wheels. She was hitting the gas and not going anywhere. Of course, if you do that long enough you wind up right where you started and out of gas.

Not long after slipping away from her mother's hospital bed, Linda began seriously questioning her approach to work and life. Seeking relevance every moment of the day had required creating a twenty-four-hour-a-day problem, and she was ready to admit that wasn't working. "I came to the conclusion that you can't chase importance," she said, "because you'll never catch it." Instead, she's trying to schedule blocks of time in her day to work without minor interruptions, and she's even going several hours without checking her messages at night. "At first it was disorienting, like I was being placed in a sensory deprivation chamber. But now I can even watch an entire movie without checking my phone—at least if it's not a long movie."

You saw the ad in the newspaper. It sounds interesting. It's an experiment on memory and learning, and they will pay you a few bucks for your time. It specifically says it's open to people from all backgrounds—accountants, plumbers, whatever you happen to do for a living.

You make an appointment and show up at an office on the local college campus. It turns out that there are two of you who will do the experiment at the same time. You both draw a slip of paper out of a box. Your slip says "teacher"; the other person gets "learner."

The task ahead is explained to you. As the teacher, you will have two duties. First, you will read various pairs of words to the learner. The learner will try to memorize those word pairs. Later, you will administer a quiz. One more thing . . . to help the learner concentrate and successfully learn the material, you will have access to an electroshock device. As the teacher, you will administer a brief shock every time the learner makes a mistake. In fact, with each additional error you will administer a higher-voltage shock. That shocking someone aids in the learning process is a premise you accept without questioning it.

You take a seat at a table, with a list of word pairs and the electroshock box in front of you. The learner is taken to the next room, where electrodes are connected to his body. Over the intercom, you begin reading the word pairs.

The electroshock box carries prominent labels. At 15 volts, the shock is labeled "slight." "Moderate" is 75 volts. At 195 volts, the shock is "very strong," progressing to "intense" at 255, "extreme" at 315, and "danger: severe" at 375 before reaching the end of the meter, 450 volts, which is labeled only "XXX."

To the learner's first mistake, you confidently turn the dial to the 15-volt shock and proceed with the next word pair. With each mistake, you are told to add an additional 15 volts. After the fifth mistake, when you dial up a 75-volt shock, you hear a grunt, the first sign of the learner's discomfort.

You confidently continue "teaching" the word pairs and raising the voltage even as the grunts turn to screams. At the tenth mistake, however, the learner begins sounding desperate. He's crying out in pain. He asks to be let out.

Your nerves begin to jump. You start to sweat. You look for guidance and are told, "Please continue." And you do.

You continue reading the lists. The learner continues to make mistakes. And you dial up increasing shocks. You start to tremble. Bite your lip. Dig your fingernails into the table.

The next shock is 315. It is labeled extreme. The learner makes another error. You pause. You are reminded, "Whether the learner likes it or not, you must go on until he has learned all the word pairs correctly, so please go on."

You laugh nervously and dial up the extreme shock.

And then. Nothing. No cries. No moans. No screams. No sounds.

Is it over? You are told it is not.

You worry what's happened to the learner. You are told again, "It is absolutely essential that we continue."

To the next word pair, you get no response. You are told to administer the shock. Again, there's no response. No cries. No whimpering. Nothing.

Again and again, no response. Finally, there is only one position left on the dial: 450 volts, or "XXX," as it is labeled. You are told to administer the maximum shock on the board.

And you do.

Though you didn't know it, the assignment of roles was rigged so that you would draw the "teacher" task. The "learner," meanwhile, was an actor. The responses were entirely scripted, from the mistaken word pairs to the screams of protest. And the experience had nothing to do with memory or learning. The point was to do see what you would do.

When psychologist Stanley Milgram designed this experiment, the experts he consulted said that there was no more than a 1-in-1,000 chance that a person would sit through this entire process and continue administering shocks in response to memory mistakes. When Milgram actually ran the experiment, 82.5 percent kept shocking after the first cries of pain, and the *majority* of participants sat in the chair and gradually upped the shocks from 15 to 450.[9]

This classic experiment is considered a warning about obedience to authority, but in reality the subjects were being obedient to a problem. What they were really responding to was the notion that the learner wouldn't succeed if he didn't receive the punishment. There is no evidence in any of the versions of this experiment that the subjects would have tortured someone just because they were told to. They were hurting people because they were seduced by the problem—unless you used this training technique, your student would never learn the lesson. They would suffer if you didn't hurt them.

Today, we have far less trust for those in positions of authority. Yet, when a researcher at Santa Clara University recently repeated the Milgram experiment, he came up with the exact same results.[10] All the evolution in our culture, all the vast differences in our relationship with authority, and the results didn't change at all. How is that possible? Because fundamentally the experiment is about how we respond to a problem. And that has not changed at all. We love problems. We lunge at problems. The problem of a learner who can't keep his word pairs straight is just as compelling to us today as it was fifty years ago—and thus we keep turning the dial.

A problem is such an invigorating force that it can distract us from our most fundamental beliefs. That was exactly Milgram's conclusion: "[O]rdinary people, simply doing their jobs, and without any particular hostility on their part, can become agents in a terrible destructive process."

WHO SEEKS POWER through problems? The short answer is everyone. Milgram showed that there wasn't any one particular group—the rich or the poor, dropouts or those with academic degrees—who wanted the power of that problem; it was every group. In fact, even people who seem to have significant power seek the consequential feeling of a good problem to tackle.

Say, for example, that a company makes two varieties of the same product. Product A is a *big* seller. However, nobody loves it. People endure it, like an obligation. Product B doesn't sell as many units, but buyers love it. They savor it. They build their day around it and they happily come back for more.

The company could go in three possible directions. It could continue to make both products, since both are profitable. It could focus on product B, since it seems likely at some point that the market will move toward the product people actually enjoy. Or there is a third option. The company could dump product B and stick with A.

Would any company stake its future on the product nobody likes, when they not only know it could be better but were actually making a better version of it at the very same time? It turns out, yes. John Pepper, CEO of the largest consumer products company in the world, did just that when he sized up the coffee market in 1992.

At the time, Procter & Gamble had two coffee divisions. One division ran factory assembly lines vacuum-packing Folgers crystals into cans for the American consumer market. The other roasted specialty arabica beans for Italian consumers and cafes.

Pepper looked at the two divisions and decided to sell off his Italian coffee operation. Why? Because it didn't make any sense to him. It didn't fit his understanding of the world. Italy was, as Pepper dismissively called it when he announced the sale, "a vastly different" coffee market.

And he was right. It was different. When Pepper and his team got up every morning in Cincinnati, Ohio, they didn't see people lining up to buy coffee at a ridiculous markup in price. They didn't see people raving about their coffee and lingering over coffee. They didn't see a coffee culture with coffee at the center of a new kind of social space.

They saw people slurp down a cup of weak coffee at home as they raced out the door. They saw people slug down another cup of weak coffee at the office. And if people went out to buy a cup of coffee in Cincinnati, they bought bad, cheap coffee in a deli and then they left, like they were supposed to. These people never said their coffee was the highlight of their day. They didn't celebrate it. They didn't venerate or mythologize it. They gulped it down and moved on.

In Italy, the coffee Procter and Gamble was making was thick, rich, and basically unrecognizable to Americans. And, oddly, a significant portion of their sales was to cafes where Italians self-indulgently went for the sole purpose of drinking coffee.

Pepper ran a company that understood soap and cleaning products and so forth—things people rely upon, things people need to have in order to accomplish basic tasks. So he looked at their two coffee operations and saw the Italian division as a luxury-selling aberration in a company that sells necessities. It was different. It didn't fit. Pepper didn't want different in his company. So he sold it off.

But as researcher Barton Weitz has pointed out in his study of the decision, this is a classic example of seeing something different as a problem instead of seeing it as an asset. For Pepper, it was a "this doesn't look right" problem—an unfamiliar market makes strange product demands, which comes to seem not just irrelevant but harmful to your overall business. Just like John Lennon's teachers, Pepper could only see the downside of something unfamiliar to him and couldn't even begin to conceive of its future.

In announcing the sale, Pepper emphasized that their Italian division was utterly disconnected and useless to their American coffee division. Weitz faults Pepper for a stunning lack of imagination. "Well, of course they are vastly different markets when you're peddling industrial freeze-dried Folgers here and fresh, exotic beans there," Weitz said. "But how long before someone figures out that if you serve people a good cup of coffee, they will literally line up out the door for it? How long before these markets come to look more alike?"

It did not take long. At exactly the same time Pepper was dismissing the idea of people actually liking his coffee, Howard Schultz was laying the foundation of the Starbucks coffee empire. Schultz took his inspiration from—of all things—the Italian coffee business, where he saw espresso bars and cafes that offered not only the quality of the drink but the romance of it. People started their day there—and then they came back later for more. They came day after day after day. And they created something there, something unique that they couldn't find in any other setting, a feeling both compelling and comfortable.

Procter and Gamble had been making Italian coffee for ten years before Howard Schultz ever set foot in Italy. They had expertise, the resources, even the coffee beans themselves. They had everything necessary to launch the future of coffee. Instead of taking what they knew from Italy and exploiting it in the United States and around the globe, they took what they assumed about the United States and saw everything else as a problematic aberration. They looked at Italy and saw peculiar people drinking peculiar coffee, and wondered why anyone would want something other than a can of Folgers. They had, within their empire, coffee that people craved and coffee that people endured, and they went for what people endured because Italy didn't fit the model and that was a problem.

Predictably, over time the market moved toward the coffee people loved. Where Folgers once made more in a day than Starbucks did in a year, Starbucks profits are now ten times larger than those of Folgers. And Procter and Gamble, surrendering against a market it could have easily devoured, wound up selling Folgers off and is now entirely out of the coffee business.

For Weitz, the lesson is obvious. "If you find yourself defining something unique as a problem," he said, "you will learn the difference the hard way."

PEOPLE USE PROBLEMS to feel consequential when they are making significant decisions, but they even fall into this trap when they are out to have fun. In fact, the appetite to tap into the power of problems can turn a pretend battle into a social war.

"It's the total immersion that draws me in," Cristina explains of her longtime hobby, historical reenactments. "The horses clatter by, kicking up the mud. The men and women speak without relying on probably ninety percent of the expressions they use in daily life. It's the smell of it, the sound of it—you are in a different time and place, and every nagging detail of your life falls away."

While reenactors are generally associated with battle scenes, Cristina's specialty is midwestern frontier life. For her, there is something intriguing about the spare and rugged existence of those who completed perilous journeys to the shores of the American land, only to keep going deeper into the unknown in search of a new world within the new world.

Though Cristina loves the adventure of it and the sense, if only for a moment, that she really has traveled through time, she laments that nobody loves to pick a fight more than a reenactor.

"You could have exactly the right clothes, I mean right down to the buttons, but if they're too clean, someone will say you're not being true to the time," Cristina said. "You could bring bales of hay for your entire village, but someone will say that they wouldn't have come tethered in that shape in the 1780s.

"Unfortunately, this hobby really lends itself to intolerance and elitism," she said. "You have the entire regular impulse to judge people magnified by the fact that everyone feels entitled to evaluate every single detail of your presentation. Like everyone here becomes judges in a beauty pageant crossed with a dog show."

Even worse are participants who portray a high-ranking character. "You show me someone playing a general, and watch out," Cristina laments. "They really get to thinking of themselves as generals, walk and talk as generals, and expect everyone to answer to them before, during, and after the reenactment. And heaven help you if you try to give them an idea or something. No good idea comes from below."

Adding to the potential for contentious condescension is the inherently imprecise nature of most everything they do. "Self-proclaimed expertise runs rampant in our set," Christina said. "Is this or that historically accurate? Well, there is no official handbook to consult. So we drown under a thousand different definitive opinions."

The reenactment culture even has its own putdown for anyone considered to be historically insufficient in some way. "We call people like that a 'farb.' We say, 'Look at that farb over there talking on his cellphone, you know, clear sins like that. But we also say someone is a farby for smelling too good," she said.

"The next thing you know, he's a farb, she's farby. Everybody's a farb or reeks of farbiness." And then, instead of time travel, it feels like Cristina's at an arbitration hearing dressed in funny clothes.

Cristina appreciates the desire to be accurate. "I read as many firsthand accounts as I can," she said. "I *try*. And we should have standards to eliminate absurd anachronisms. But if you go back before the 1820s there are no photographs, and it's not hard to figure out that even when you have a painting or two of a historical event, some of those painters took some pretty big liberties in turning what they saw into what they drew."

Cristina wants her fellow hobbyists to lose their impulse to put people down and be dismissive toward them. "Nobody enjoys the experience and nobody really learns from it. We have to move toward being accurate without attacking each other. We can have high standards without elitism. Otherwise, really, what's the point," she asks. "I mean, we could skip all the history and the horses and the mud and the tents, and just walk around insulting each other, like high school."

THE TAKEAWAY

Call him a problem, and suddenly your teaching skills are relevant to this vexing child named John Lennon. Call it a problem, and don't learn a single thing from the Italian coffee market, and Procter and Gamble can reassert that its industrial coffee is best. Call them problems—or, in reenactor-speak, *farbs*—and your clothes, and your speech, and your hay bales look better than someone else's. Chase every problem you can find, and you can consider yourself essential every single minute on the job. Call it a problem when someone can't memorize a list, and you can inflict punishment and make him or her better.

No matter the context, with a problem in hand, we matter. With a problem we are consequential. With a problem, attention must be paid. And so we relentlessly chase problems to make ourselves seem bigger.

We believe in throwing ourselves at problems so fervently that **82.5 percent of us would physically hurt someone to teach him or her a lesson.**

With a problem in hand, it's like we're looking at ourselves in a fun-house mirror while trying to put makeup on. We look a lot bigger to ourselves that way—but to everyone else we look like we're just making a mess.

TWO FOR THE ROAD: PUTTING POWER PROBLEMS IN THEIR PLACE

Take less. Al Franken's big break in comedy came with a catch. Along with his comedy partner, Tom Davis, he had landed a dream job offer from *Saturday Night Live*. The producers told him they loved the material and wanted to hire them both as writers. But, as a comedy writing team, Franken and Davis were offered only one writer's salary—if they wanted the job they would have to work for what amounted to half pay. The power problem play would have been to walk away. It was insulting to be treated like half a person. But Franken recognized that working on the show would likely transform his career. Indeed, he says today that he owes everything in his improbable career that took him from comedy to the U.S. Senate to once being willing to work for half pay. As practice against the power problem trap, take less of something today, even if it's just the smaller half when you break a cookie in two.

— — — — — — — —

Go look at an abstract painting. We don't do well with uncertainty and ambiguity. We fight it. Run from it. It makes us feel power*less*. It makes us throw a bad decision at a problem just for the sake of feeling stronger. But transformative decisions are almost always the product of mastering uncertainty and embracing ambiguity. How do people get better at this? Go look at some works of abstract art. Go to a museum, crack open an art book, or just search for them online. Look at paintings by Jackson Pollock or Frank Stella, or any work of art that isn't a literal representation of something. Researchers have found that abstract art inspires unease, uncertainty, and a reaction not unlike fright.[3] But if you can overcome that impulse to turn away from the discomfort in art, you will have an easier time tolerating uncertainty in daily life without creating problems.

CHAPTER 4

- - - - - - - - - -

Don't Come Home
for Christmas and Other
Lessons on Trying Harder
and Making It Worse

WHAT IF YOU actually watched a pot? Would it ever boil? Of course it would. But there's wisdom in the old saying anyway. Because no amount of watching, no sense of urgency, no investment of your time focused on the pot will have the slightest positive effect. Your effort contributes nothing. But watching the pot does make it seem to take longer to boil and keeps you from doing anything useful.

We understand that when it comes to pots and water, but we forget it when it comes to everything else. Think about what every coach you've ever had has told you: Try harder. What every teacher you have ever had has told you: Try harder. What your parents, your boss, and Dear Abby told you: Try harder. It is received wisdom that the difference between winning and losing is effort.

But effort and incentives focus our attention on the problem at hand. Focusing on the nonboiling pot doesn't make it boil. And focusing on whatever problem we are having doesn't fix the problem. In fact, high effort and high incentives make us more likely to get frustrated and less likely to persist.

Focusing on a problem is an unproductive habit. But it's a habit that draws us in, because problems are compelling. Paying attention to problems makes us feel like we are repelling a significant threat and that we are of consequence. The power of problems over us is only compounded by the fact that our favorite remedies actually make our problems worse. We take our problems and douse them in Miracle-Gro until they are so big we can't lift them.

First among those ill-chosen remedies is effort.

It's not that people should give up, never try, never apply themselves. The point is simply this: Turning effort up to an 11 on a 10-point scale is inherently counterproductive—it makes our problems seem bigger and our abilities seem smaller.

BUD MEYER BELIEVED in effort with the fervor of a preacher. Hard work, he said, solves every problem.

Bud Meyer applied that philosophy to his work as a chemical engineer and to the upbringing of his children, including his son Urban.

When Urban Meyer disappointed his father by striking out in a high school baseball game, Bud told him that he was unwelcome in the family car. So Urban Meyer walked home. It was ten miles away.

Happily, Urban was a star shortstop for the team and didn't strike out very often. And, by the end of his senior season scouts from major league teams were buzzing around him, thinking he might have the potential to be a major leaguer.

Days after high school graduation, the Atlanta Braves signed Urban to a contract and shipped him off to rookie ball, the lowest level of minor league baseball.

In rookie ball, Urban Meyer floundered. The Braves tried him at shortstop, second base, third, and even as a catcher, but no matter where they put him, he couldn't hit at that level of competition and he couldn't field. Urban—a seventeen-year-old playing minor league baseball 1,200 miles from home—called Bud every night with another unhappy recap of his game. Finally, Urban told Bud that he couldn't hack it, and that it was time for him to give up the baseball dream.

Failure was a problem for Bud, of course. And that problem was to be met with pure effort, nothing less. So Bud told Urban that if he quit, Bud never wanted to see him again. Never. Urban would be permanently unwelcome in the Meyer family home. Urban could call his mother once a year on Christmas, but when he did Bud would not be coming to the phone.

Urban didn't quit. Bud's words echoed in his mind amid the sweat and the strikeouts and the long bus rides between road games. He played out his first and then second minor league seasons—both in rookie ball—and then the Braves unceremoniously released him from his contract. He was no longer a baseball player, but you could not say he hadn't tried his hardest.

Ninety-nine percent of high school baseball players do not make it as far as Urban Meyer did in the game. But no amount of effort or shame was going to carry him any farther. He did not have the tools to progress up the minor league baseball ladder, much less to make major league baseball.

Urban, however, was not through with sports. After an unimpressive stint playing college football, he began a coaching career that would one day take him to the top of the college football profession, winning two national championships at the University of Florida.

After the first national championship, Bud was asked what he thought of his son's coaching success. "I wouldn't say I'm agog about it," he replied. "He's performed in a way that is expected."

Far from being critical of his father's zealous belief in total effort, Urban himself was quick to credit his father's teachings for his professional success. He lived Bud's lessons and he was still welcome in his father's home. No one could outwork him.

However, it was Urban's all-encompassing effort that nearly drove him from the game.

At the University of Florida, one of the most important and cherished rituals Urban initiated was called Victory Meal. After a win, and only after wins, the entire team gathered for a jubilant postgame dinner. Looming over the dinner table were giant televisions, each showing a replay of the game. The meal was a reward, a celebration, a chance to strengthen bonds across the team, and a means to show what they were all playing for—a team that was larger than each individual member but that thrived as one. No one would dare miss the meal—it was what they played for.

As the winning seasons piled up, Urban began skipping some Victory Meals so that he could get a few hours more work done preparing for the next game. As he sought a second national championship, he stopped going entirely.

A few years later he ducked his head into a Victory Meal on his way to his office to watch some game film. Opening the door, he was shocked by the quiet. As he stepped inside, he saw why it was so quiet. The room was nearly deserted. Most of the tables were entirely untouched. Just a handful of players and two assistant coaches were quietly eating dinner.

Where is everyone, he asked? Reluctantly, his conditioning coach revealed that when Urban stopped coming to Victory Meal, so did almost all the players.

Urban was pained that in the name of working hard to advance the team, he had undermined his own team-building effort. Suddenly it seemed that perhaps perfect effort was not the perfect plan, and that meeting every problem with more effort came at an unanticipated cost. He wondered for the first time since he'd been left to walk home from that baseball game: Was there maybe something other than a straight line between effort and victory?

Within a few weeks, philosophical concerns gave way to something far more alarming. Urban was lying in bed struggling to breathe. There was a pain in his chest. He rolled out of bed but couldn't get himself off the floor. As his wife dialed 911, Urban Meyer thought he was having a heart attack.

While the episode was terribly frightening for the family, doctors said that he had not suffered a heart attack. Instead, the stress and unhealthy habits that accompany twenty-hour workdays had simply overwhelmed him.

Convinced now that being the hardest-working football coach in America was a threat rather than an accomplishment, Urban walked away from one of the biggest contracts in the game and declared himself retired at the age of 46.

With time to reflect about the way he pursued his work, Urban came to believe his all-out effort had hurt his team, himself, and most importantly his family. He ultimately agreed to come back to football—to head one of the most storied programs in the game, at Ohio State—but did so only after signing a contract with his family. He agreed to set maximum work hours and minimum family time in his weekly schedule. He agreed to follow various rules to protect his health and mental well-being. And he agreed that bottomless effort was not what was going to make his football team successful.

Urban now quotes a passage from a management handbook that asks, "Why do people persist in their self-destructive behavior, ignoring the blatant fact that what they've been doing for many years hasn't solved their problems? They think that they need to do it even more fervently or frequently, as if they were doing the right thing but simply had to try even harder."

As he quotes the book, and reimagines his approach to work, the echoes of Bud's exhortations to "try harder or you won't be welcome home" grow fainter. Urban saw that effort was the thing that cost him his job at Florida, and that effort nearly kept his family from wanting to come to Ohio State. Effort came at the cost of the Victory Meal and commitments that weren't hard work but were just as important. Ultimately, he saw that the mentality that there can be no limit on effort imposes a limit on everything else.

If you were to look up the concept of self-defeating effort, "it should have my picture," Urban tells people now. "Because that's exactly what happened."

Though it says on her business card that she's a writing coach, Sharon thinks of herself as part coach, part teacher, part psychologist, and part social worker. "I'm the person you call when it's time to pick up the pieces because you'd rather do anything but write," Sharon says.

Sharon's clients tend to view writing as the hardest thing they have to do. "They look at the blank screen, or the blank piece of paper, and it just induces this sense of panic and despair," she says. "And it is such a perfect catalyst for procrastination. What's the harm if I just take a minute to look up that friend from the fourth grade I haven't seen in thirty years, or check to see if the lint catcher in the dryer is empty, or call the people in human resources and see if my W-2 is up to date?"

When her clients are in the worst shape, they tend to see every word they have to write as being like lifting a heavy stone. "After they lift that stone, they're not even sure it was the right one, or if it will stand," she says. "And if just one topples, the whole thing comes down on them."

Sharon works with many different kinds of writers—students writing essays for school, technical writers who have to master the language of an industry, and aspiring professional fiction and nonfiction writers. What her clients tend to have in common—whether they are writing their first 500-word essay or they write for a living—is what she calls unbalanced attention.

"Much of the teaching of writing is the imposition of

standards," she says. "We say, 'This is what good writing looks like.' Now, naturally, you hold that example in your head when you write or when you try to write."

The process intimidates writers because the standards are all but impossible to meet. "Then, the more you care, the harder you work, the more frustrated you become," she says, "because you've invested so much in what you're doing, and you still don't feel it's equal to what good writing is supposed to be."

As if we were all taught writing by Bud Meyer, Sharon says the typical response to this problem is to redouble your efforts. "Now you've worked even harder, and the problem is even worse."

Sharon had a client say to her once that she knew so many rules of writing that she could not sit down and write a sentence anymore. "That's the heart of it. We feel like the harder we work at something, the more natural it will feel to us," she says. "But you can work harder and harder on writing only to have it feel more foreign because you accumulate all these rules and standards and now every single word seems out of place."

Sharon keeps a journal that she fills with great writing advice. One page she's highlighted and underlined and put stars next to contains a quote from *Slaughterhouse-Five* author Kurt Vonnegut. Vonnegut warned: "Good Taste will put you out of business."

Sharon knows that Vonnegut went on to advise prospective writers to drop out of school before they could be filled with all that good taste and taught conclusively that they were incapable of demonstrating it. Vonnegut himself considered it a stroke of luck that he studied science and anthropology in college—since he hadn't studied writing, no one had a chance to teach him that he wasn't capable of doing it.

Sharon can't erase all the lessons her clients have already absorbed, of course. What she does, however, is try to get her clients to play with writing instead of work at it.

"I will sit down with clients and hand them a piece of paper and a pencil and say write something about this pencil, or about this room, or about your hand, or about the weather. It is always something very accessible and immediate," Sharon explained. "And I will say, 'There are no rules. No standards. And whatever you write, I'm going to crumple it up and throw it out.'"

There's really only one thing Sharon is looking for in this exercise—and she almost always gets it. "I'm looking for a smile. I'm looking for a break in the dam that's been holding them up from writing freely, from enjoying writing," she says. "There's something in the absurdity of the topic, in something silly they've written, and it just opens up the process for them."

She continues a series of exercises emphasizing that it's not how hard you try and it's not how many rules you know. "Writing, like anything else vital in life, is better when it's natural," Sharon said. Much like Urban Meyer's journey to a new perspective on good work habits, Sharon tries to get her clients to a point where their efforts are natural and human instead of obsessive and robotic.

There's an old gimmick in golf if you really want to befuddle another player. Just before they hit the ball, ask them if they inhale or exhale when they take their backswing. They'll say they don't know. And then, instead of swinging naturally, they'll be thinking about how to properly breathe. "That's the essence of good writing," Sharon says. "If you're thinking about the specifics, then you're not doing it. If you are thinking about writing, you're not writing. If I can get you to just do it, so to speak, then I've made you a better writer, a person capable of creating something you will love."

When you come into the office for the study, you find a table, bare of anything except what appears to be some kind of puzzle made out of wooden blocks, a set of diagrams, and some magazines.

You are told that you will be asked to fit the puzzle pieces together and configure them into various shapes. Diagrams of those shapes are laid out in front of you. After a practice run, the researcher tells you that he will be watching from behind a two-way mirror and measuring how long it takes you to construct each shape.

It takes you a while, but you figure out how to build the first shape. And then the second, third, and fourth. After you finish building four different designs, the researcher comes out and says you are almost finished. He just needs to retrieve a form for you to fill out, and then you will be done.

With the researcher heading out the door and down the hall, what do you do? You have the blocks. You have several diagrams you haven't used yet. You could try to figure out some more shapes. You could just sit there, or you could peruse one of the magazines—*Time*, *The New Yorker*, and *Playboy* are sitting right next to you.

You didn't know it, but there was a second researcher, behind the glass, watching what you did in this moment. In fact, the entire point of the experiment was this moment. Did you want to make more puzzle shapes, or did you abandon all that now in favor of current events, witty cartoons, or pictures of naked women?

It turns out that there was one big difference between the people who picked up the magazines and the people who kept building puzzles. If the researcher said that he was paying you for successfully completing the puzzles, you were twice as likely to put the puzzle down immediately after the researcher left. If there had been no money offered for your puzzle skills, you were more likely to keep working on the puzzle even when you thought you were alone and the puzzle-building task was over.[1]

The same pattern emerged in the punishment version of the experiment. Here, people who failed to finish a puzzle within the time available were subjected to an air horn that was jarringly loud and unpleasant. Working against this negative inducement, you put the puzzle down and reached for a magazine the moment the task was finished. If there was no threat of punishment, *Time*, *Playboy*, and *The New Yorker* were happily left to the side while you tried to figure out the other puzzle designs.

Why did clear, concrete incentives fail to make you more committed to and interested in successfully completing the puzzles? Edward Deci, the researcher who dreamed up these experiments, concluded that there is an intrinsic interest, a sort of gut-level interest, that ultimately guides our attentions. And when we try to alter that gut-level response with inducements, we have the opposite of the intended effect. Instead of making something more interesting, more vital, more alive, we transform it into a bloodless transaction that we wish to rid ourselves of at the first opportunity.

Deci repeated the basic experiment in many ways, always coming to the same conclusion. Curious whether this same pattern was visible outside the context of puzzles and laboratories, he ran a version of the experiment at a college newspaper.

Without anyone other than the editor knowing what was going on, Deci's researcher was introduced to the staff as a new assistant editor. Among other tasks, the researcher was in charge of the team of students who wrote headlines.

Here, Deci took advantage of the fact that the newspaper was published twice a week and had two different teams of headline writers. He decided to pay Team 1 based on its productivity, while Team 2 received no bonus for extra work.

Just as in the puzzle experiment, the college newspaper staff was repulsed by the incentives. In return for its productivity bonus, Team 1 was less productive per hour worked and missed more days of work.[2]

Deci concluded that there is a giant hole in the equation Incentive + Harder Work = Better Outcome. That is, incentives don't produce harder work, and harder work doesn't produce better outcomes. An engaged mind beats the best incentive and the hardest worker every time. Engagement is sustaining, he said, while incentives and pure effort are limiting.

"Never underestimate the power of a person intrigued by a task, and never overestimate the value of a person with a task incentive," Deci said. "Whether leading a group or motivating yourself—make it a puzzle you want to solve and you can do more than you ever set out to accomplish. Work hard to come up with a system of rewards and punishments and as fast as you go you will never take a step beyond the finish line."

FOR MICHELE AND Erik, it started small—as these things do. Almost imperceptibly, their fifteen-year-old son Brandon became gradually less reliable. Instead of mowing the lawn like he was supposed to, you had to ask him a second, third, and fourth time. The trigonometry homework that he said was finished yesterday afternoon is suddenly not finished at breakfast the next morning, and now he's racing to make sense of cosines and tangents while spilling Honey Nut Cheerios on his papers.

It was hardly the end of the world, but Michele and Erik were concerned. If this carelessness became a way of life, what would that mean for getting into college? For getting through it? For jobs and life and everything. "You don't want to overreact," Michele said, "but it's hard not to worry that if he stops doing easy things, what's going to happen when life demands hard things from him?"

So Michele and Erik set up a chart with categories, including doing his regular chores, finishing his homework and keeping up his grades, and being on time for dinner. They built in some small inducements for meeting all the standards each week, like a gift card for downloading music.

While they had meant for the chart to be a means of encouraging good behavior, it rapidly turned into something of a scorecard, a running ledger of what went right and what didn't. With the chart in hand they could easily compare one week to the next. Unaware that Edward Deci's research suggests their efforts to make things better would likely make things worse, they were stunned when they looked at the numbers and saw that their new tracking and incentive system had exactly the opposite of the intended effect.

"You could just count the check marks each week, and they didn't go straight down, but close to it," Erik said. "It would have seemed like a great success if the goal was to get him to stop doing his homework and always be late."

"What's he thinking in there?" Erik wondered. "It's really hard to know. You ask him if he's going to do something, he always says yes. You ask him if he understands what we expect of him, he always says yes. But then he doesn't do it."

More troubling to Michele and Erik, Brandon started to act like there were no rules. "He came home one Saturday night four hours past the time we told him to be in by. That's not going to fly," Michele said.

Just as Sharon's students did, just as Bud Meyer taught, Michele and Erik decided that when at first you don't succeed, try harder. They took the failure of their plan as evidence that they needed to do more. So they upped the rewards and added a punishment category. They expanded the list of expected behaviors and lengthened the timeline. Miss a standard and you're staying home Saturday night, or any one of various pieces of electronics are going away, or a summer of extra SAT tutoring awaits. Hit enough standards over a long enough period of time and there's an iPad coming, or a used car when Brandon turns sixteen.

Much to their surprise, the new system produced no more desired results than the old one. "We tried to pile on everything we thought was important—good or bad—to him, and it was as if we hadn't done anything at all," Erik said.

"It doesn't seem rational," Erik said. "The way I see things, you want something, you have to do A, B, and C for it, then you do A, B, and C."

In talking to friends who had teenagers, Michele and Erik found out that they were hardly alone in coming up with ineffective ways to encourage good behavior.

"It could be girls, or grades, or games," Michele said, "the problems or combinations of problems can be different, but the result is almost always the same. You set up some kind of rules about what's acceptable, you establish some kind of inducement toward what you want to have happen, and then you see all that ignored."

Michele came to realize the futility of their efforts when she and Brandon happened to see a television ad for one of those magic slicer-dicers. "The kind where you somehow can peel things in one stroke, and it comes out perfect," Michele explained. "And he said, 'We should get that.' And I said, 'It's overpriced junk.' And he said, 'We should get that.' I thought to myself, 'We're really not seeing the same world out there.'"

From that Michele began to consider what she decided might be the fundamental problem with their charts and incentives. "We were basically pretending that Brandon is making a decision like a banker or something, thinking about the value of what we were offering," she said. "But you can't sell long-term thinking to teenagers, who are pretty much the definition of people who think for the short term.

"We came to conclude that no amount of pushing was going to solve this problem," she added.

The charts came down, the iPad offer expired, and Michele and Erik took a new approach. They didn't try as hard to get what they wanted, and they were rewarded for it.

"We sat down with Brandon and said we need to be able to count on you," Michele said. "So we told him the things we needed him to never falter on, and we said there were some things where we could cut him some slack. And things started to get a little better from there."

IN THE 1940s, the smoke jumpers of the U.S. Forest Service were an elite team of professional adventurers ready to do battle with fire—not with water but with only their wits and the most rudimentary tools. They stood ready at a moment's notice to jump on a plane and, more to the point, to jump off it and into harm's way.

Their job was to get there early, block the fire's path, and keep small fires from becoming big fires. That was their plan when a lightning strike started a fire near Mann Gulch, deep in the Montana wilderness.

Though they lost their ability to communicate with their command center when they threw the radio out of the plane and its parachute failed to open, the team took that as a minor setback. They thought this one had all the appearances of what they called a "10 o'clock fire," the kind that they would have completely under control by the next morning. In fact, the first thing they did when they landed was open up their sacks and sit down for lunch.

After the meal, their assumptions quickly melted away. Landing on what they thought was the safe side of Mann Gulch, they came to realize that the fire had jumped the gulch.

A plan for fighting the fire quickly gave way as foreman Wag Dodge called for a full retreat.

But the grass was tall. Men move slowly when they are carrying their gear, moving in grass that is two or three feet tall, and heading up a hill. Fire moves faster.

Dodge realized that they would not win the race carrying their equipment, so he ordered everyone to drop their tools. But his men wouldn't do it. It cut against their creed. The tools were a part of them, who they are, why they were there. With the tools, they were smoke jumpers; without tools, they were just another group of helpless sightseers out where they shouldn't be.

Like boys who wouldn't be welcome home for Christmas if they didn't try, these men simply worked harder, racing against the fire, seeking a point where they could make their stand against it. The fire was a problem, and you meet a problem with maximum effort. That was the only way to fight a fire, they well knew. There was no room for weakness out there.

Desperate to keep his stubborn men from running a race they could not win, Dodge issued a new order. They would build their own fire. They would burn out a small area—creating a space where the fire would find no fuel—and then they would crouch down in that space and hope the real fire would pass over them. It was, at minimum, a chance to decide when the fire would reach them, instead of almost certainly being overtaken at a moment of the fire's choosing.

Smoke jumpers set fires all the time. One of their tactics in fighting fires was to set a back fire to control the direction of the wildfire. But in this case, there was no time to do any of that—all Dodge's plan would do was clear a small escape hatch within the flames.

To that, his men objected. Setting a fire was a tactic for

stopping a fire, nothing else, they believed. And thus with the most severe incentive imaginable, the men were uselessly obsessed with trying harder. Instead of seeing Dodge's order as an act of creative genius, they thought he was weak or they thought he was nuts. Either way, he could no longer think straight and was therefore no longer to be obeyed.

While Dodge carried out his plan, setting his fire and clearing a space to hide in, his men clutched their equipment and kept running.

Dodge's plan worked. After the fire had passed over him, Dodge stood on ground on which there was nothing left to burn. He was now safe, but where were his men? He began a search. Out of his team of fifteen men, two had survived.

There are few more poignant examples of the true value of effort. Pure effort, by itself, can be useless. Indeed, it can be harmful. Dodge lay down in the soot and the ash and the dirt. He hid from an unstoppable enemy, and lived to fight it another day. His colleagues saw the fire as a problem to be met with maximum effort, so they expended every ounce of energy they had moving as fast as they could carrying heavy tools to the very end. They worked as hard as they could until they destroyed themselves with their effort.

The smoke jumpers died carrying their tools up a hill, when their tools were beyond useless to them. They died because they didn't want to fail at fighting the fire, but survival was the only way they could ever succeed. They clung to their understanding of the problem instead of trying a solution that fit the situation they were in—and the decision killed them. If that level of incentive and effort doesn't inspire a clear look at things, then no amount of incentive and effort ever will.

The Takeaway

It's so obvious we would never stop to even question it. What should we do if we are struggling with a problem? Try harder. What should we do if we absolutely need to come out on top? Raise the stakes, create incentives, and put our total focus on the issue. And when we do all that, it has one clear effect: It makes our problems worse.

With the smoke jumpers' lives on the line, with Urban Meyer's career on the line, total, all-out effort was a threat and a hindrance. Effort ties Sharon's writing students in knots and left Michele and Erik wondering how they had worked so hard to come up with a system that only made their teenager less reliable. What they all had in common was belief in the very alluring notion that all-out effort is the purest pursuit of success. But as Edward Deci's experiments showed, forced effort fails against natural curiosity every time. **We are twice as likely to stick to a challenge without an incentive.**

Maximizing effort is a fool's comfort. We burn out, we make illogical decisions, we don't build engagement with the task. It's a comforting response, but it's a wrong one.

We've all seen this firsthand. There's a tiny stain on your shirt—so small you can barely see it. It's annoying, though. Probably best to leave it alone. But. If you could just get it off, *that* would be better. You try to flick it off with a fingernail. Doesn't work. You go at it with a napkin and some water. Now the stain is bigger. It's ground in. There's no getting it out. And instead of something tiny and obscure, you've created this massive dark spot on your shirt that people can see from across the room. You gave it your all, and you made it worse.

There's a reason we go at those stains and make the problem worse. We have to try harder. It's what we've been taught. It's what we believe. But it just doesn't work.

Two for the Road: How to Put Outcomes over Effort

Skip practice. When something is important, we want to prepare more thoroughly. But going over and over something in advance tends to lock us into one way of seeing and doing, while simultaneously stamping out spontaneity and possibility. That is why Bruce Springsteen likes to record his songs *before* his band fully knows the music. "If people learn their parts too well," he said, "they consciously perform rather than flat-out play." When he hears his band come alive in the studio, even if it's a bit rough around the edges, he holds up his hands and says, "That's good. If it gets any better than that, it'll be worse."

- - - - - - - -

Slow down. People think the only way to exercise properly is to go at it full tilt. In fact, researchers have found that we vastly overestimate the number of calories burned from running fast—and underestimate the number of calories burned from running slowly.[3] Unfortunately, many people give up on exercise because they can't run fast and don't realize they would do themselves more good running slowly anyway. The same logic applies to whatever you are doing. We overvalue speed in almost everything we are doing—because we associate speed with effort. But hurrying wears us down and closes out possibilities. Slow down in something you do today and see how much more you can get out of it.

CHAPTER 5

- - - - - - - - - - -

Would You Get on
the Bus to Abilene?

WHAT IF WE all decide to get on the bus to Abilene?

That was the odd question that confronted a generation of U.S. Army officers after they sat through a management training video. In the video, a family sits on their porch on a hot summer day. One after another, members of the family say, "I'm bored" and "I'm bored too." In an effort to stave off the torpor, the family heads to the bus station. They wind up finding seats on a bus to Abilene. When they finally get there, somebody says, "You know, I didn't really want to go to Abilene." And then the next person says, "I didn't want to go; I thought you wanted to go," and so on around the group. It becomes abundantly clear that *no one* in the family wanted to go to Abilene.

For the officers who watched it, some forced to endure it several times, the story served as a succinct and memorable warning about group decision making. A group of reasonable people can make a senseless, unreasonable decision. A group can unanimously support a decision that no individual member of the group would have supported alone. A group is not just the addition of all its members' capabilities; sometimes it represents a division into something less than what a single member could accomplish.

The training video story lingered in those officers' memories and would pop back into mind any time they saw a group careening toward a bad decision. In fact, they merely had to say the words "I think we're all getting on the bus to Abilene here" to get their colleagues to slow down.

Now, there is a reason that the gleaming conference tables where very important decisions are made are surrounded by many chairs. The reason is: We believe bigger is better. We have been taught that bigger is better. No one ever told us that the way to solve something is to put *fewer* people on the case.

But a group suffers from the same limitations that we face as individuals. If an individual tends to focus on a problem and not the solution, a group displays the exact same trait. In fact, the group dynamic can be far worse, as it solidifies a collective focus on a particular aspect of the problem and makes that problem all the more disruptive.

Frederick Brooks memorably warned the computer industry, "Adding manpower to a late software project makes it later." That reality applies to any aspect of work or life. You don't find a solution by throwing people at the problem. What you find with more people are more problems.

WHEN SHE WAS in high school, Katherine Bomkamp spent many hours in places like the waiting area of Walter Reed

Army Medical Center. While her father, a disabled veteran, was receiving treatment, Katherine would talk to the injured service members who were waiting nearby for their doctor's appointments.

She asked them how they were. She wasn't looking for them to say "fine"; she really wanted to know. She asked them about their injuries, their rehabilitation, what they were going through, what they needed help with. While almost everyone else shied away from asking about their pain, Katherine was direct.

You had to be strong to ask those questions and accept the answers without flinching. The soldiers she met were just back from the wars in Iraq and Afghanistan, and the injuries they had suffered were often devastating. She was supportive and caring and probably did more good than she could imagine merely by letting the soldiers tell her the truth about their struggles.

It was heartbreaking and touching at the same time. But after hearing the same concern from several soldiers, Katherine wanted to do something more than lend a sympathetic ear. She wondered what she could do that would really make a difference for the soldiers who had lost limbs in the war. These soldiers kept telling her the same thing: One of the most painful, frightening, and disorienting problems they experienced was phantom limb pain. "When they told me their stories, that just kept coming up," Katherine said.

Our brains are wired to control our limbs. Even when the limb is lost, the brain continues to do its job, sending out signals telling the missing limb what to do. In the jumble of misfired signals, the brain creates very real pain trying to connect with a limb that no longer exists.

The soldiers told her that the doctors' answer to phantom limb pain was to prescribe pills—powerful antipsychotics and barbiturates. Judging from what the soldiers told her and everything she read about the subject later, it was obvious to Katherine that even if the pills helped with the phantom limb pain, they were causing their own terrible side effects. Antipsychotics left many soldiers impotent and lethargic and dealing with a host of other new issues, while the barbiturates' main effect on soldiers was to get them hooked on barbiturates.

"These soldiers lost part of their bodies for us," Katherine said. "And instead of helping them, they were being given pills that just created new problems for them."

The basic logic of it didn't make sense to Katherine. A soldier who lost a leg didn't need a pill that changed the way his brain related to his whole body—he needed a treatment that was targeted to his actual injury.

Katherine wondered how such an important and terrible affliction could be addressed with such a weak response. She thought that there had to be a better solution. A solution that doesn't hurt more than it helps. Why hadn't the doctors at Walter Reed and every other military hospital come up with something better? Where were the university researchers? Where were the medical device companies? Where is the know-how of a military with two million soldiers? Why haven't they thought of something better when the soldiers to whom we owe so much needed science to come through for them? Of course, all these institutions knew a great deal about the problem of phantom limb pain. But inside the problem they didn't see a solution.

Katherine could not understand why all these giant organizations were failing when it came to this, but she decided she would just have to take phantom limb pain on by herself. She was a high school student with no special knowledge of or interest in science or medicine or orthotics. But she cared about those injured warriors she met, and she believed there was a better answer. And so when her classmates were busying themselves with model volcanoes and hamsters in a maze, Katherine's project for her high school science fair was treating phantom limb pain.

Katherine's approach was centered on one key idea: distraction. "If I could somehow interrupt the body's communication with the missing limb, distract it from the effort to control the limb, then maybe I could make the pain go away," she thought.

With distraction as the goal, Katherine quickly settled on the power of heat to attract the brain's attention. She wondered if a heated prosthetic would make the brain focus on responding to the heat instead of sending signals to the absent limb.

She jury-rigged an example with store-bought supplies and briefly tested it with some soldiers she had met at the army hospital. They were thrilled she was trying to help them. She was thrilled when the feedback was positive.

Committed to taking her idea as far as she possibly could, she asked professors at a local college to help her create her own crash course in electrical engineering. And with that, she was off and running trying to build a full prototype of her heated prosthetic.

Armed with working knowledge of how to create a safe and durable heating element, she needed a real prosthetic to work with to see if she could successfully work her insight into the design of an existing device. She found a directory of prosthetic companies and called them one by one. Could they provide her with a leg she could use for testing? Were they interested in working with her? Before she could describe the work she had done, the courses she had taken, her theory, her initial results or any of that, she was met with immediate dismissal. They heard a girl who wasn't in the industry and wasn't even out of high school, and they didn't need to hear any more. "A lot of people hung up on me," Katherine said. They told her, "This won't work, you're just a kid, don't waste my time."

When she finally found a company willing to listen, she was on her way. From high school and now into college, Katherine has continued to work on her device. Testing continues to go well, and she has a patent pending. Her current version even allows the user to control the temperature of the prosthetic with a smartphone.

Her work has brought her personal rewards. She started a company to build the device. She was the youngest person ever invited to speak at the Royal Society of Medicine's Innovations Summit in London. And yes, she won the science fair. And she is grateful for all of it. But more importantly, she's building a product to help those soldiers she met at Walter Reed.

It stung that so many prosthetic companies immediately wrote her off. But she takes it as a major life lesson that she didn't listen to them. "When a big company tells you no, it doesn't mean you're wrong," Katherine now tells her fellow students in an entrepreneurship program. "It may mean you're so right they can't even see it."

WHEN ROBERT REICH became the U.S. Secretary of Labor, he took over a department with seventeen thousand employees, a budget of ten billion dollars, and responsibilities for ensuring workplace safety, providing job training to the underskilled, and enforcing wage and benefit rules and all manner of other workplace laws. As if mastering the sheer size of the place was not daunting enough, there was the political climate to contend with, including no shortage of internal and external challenges to the department's mission. It was, in short, a difficult assignment. And it wasn't made any easier by the fact that Reich's previous job was as a professor, where he spent his time teaching and squirreled away in his office writing studies on the Japanese economy. He came to the office, then, with a lot of theories about the labor market and not a whit of experience running the Labor Department or anything at all, for that matter.

To compensate for the enormity of the task at hand, cabinet secretaries are provided a large personal staff whose entire job is to help the secretary do his job. The first few months were a whirlwind for Reich. He was navigating through his own department, reaching out to major constituencies the department serves, speaking at events across the country, and fighting a seemingly endless battle to win the support of his own president for budget items he considered essential.

In the midst of it all, Reich was struck by the fact that nobody had ever once asked him how he wanted to spend his day, where he wanted to go, with whom he wanted to speak. How exactly, he wondered, did all these speaking engagements and other commitments that filled his day make it onto his daily schedule?

Reich hit the intercom and summoned his assistants. "How do you know what to put on my schedule?" he asked.

They were taken aback. They assumed he knew. But they patiently explained it to him anyway. "We have you do and see what you'd choose if you had time to examine all the options yourself—sifting through all the phone calls, letters, memos, and meeting invitations," one assistant told him.

His team assumed Reich would immediately see the logic in this. A cabinet secretary can't very well spend all his time deciding how to spend his time. That would be absurd.

But Reich was still puzzled. How could they possibly know what he would choose to do?

They answered with the perfect Washington insider response, "Don't worry, we know."

Reich trusted his team. He believed they all shared his core values and all very much belonged working in the Department of Labor. But he was flabbergasted that his team had built a bubble around him.

"They transmit to me through the bubble only those letters, phone calls, memoranda, people, meetings, and events which they believe someone like me ought to have," he later recounted. "But if I see and hear only what 'someone like me' should see and hear, no original or out-of-the-ordinary thought will ever permeate the bubble. I'll never be surprised or shocked. I'll never be forced to rethink or reevaluate anything. I'll just lumber along, blissfully ignorant of what I really need to see and hear—which are things that don't merely confirm my preconceptions about the world."

His team was unimpressed by his concerns. The five guardians of his bubble told him that the bubble protected him from people who would waste his time, harass him, and otherwise serve him no good purpose.

The problem his team was addressing made perfect sense to

them. They were guardians of his time, and they intended to ensure that his limited time was focused on the right tasks. But Reich saw the consequences of their plan clearly. If his time was always spent doing things that were pleasing to him, he would never accomplish much of anything or solve anything because he would never get his hands dirty. That attitude, that commitment to see to it that only good things came his way, would be admirable if they were parenting a two-year-old, Reich told them, but they were serving the Department of Labor.

While Katherine Bomkamp had to fend off a group that offered only reflexive rejection of her ideas, Robert Reich faced the opposite issue. His group offered him only reflexive praise. Either way, it was a closed loop that cut off information and shut down the path to potential new answers.

Reich understood he could not offer any real leadership in an echo chamber, so he instituted a new rule.

He told his team that instead of reading only the mail that was complimentary, from now on he wanted to see the "mean, ass-kicking letters" too. He also wanted direct access to Department of Labor employee complaints. He wanted to be informed of bad news in real time and wanted to hold a series of open meetings at which people the department served could ask anything they wanted of him. And he wanted to see business leaders and business organizations on his schedule every week. They would almost certainly tell Reich he was wrong, but he wanted to hear it, and wanted to see if he could change a few minds.

YOU COME UP the stairs and see a group of eight people milling around in the hallway, waiting. You stand among them for a minute.

The researcher comes through, unlocks the door, and asks everyone to take a seat. There are exactly enough seats for the people in the room. Quickly, the only seat left open to you is the second one from the back.

The researcher explains the task. This is a study of visual perception, he says. Everyone in the group will be looking at the same things and will be responding aloud to all questions.

There will be, the researcher explained, two placards at the front of the room. On the left will be a single line. On the right, three lines, numbered 1, 2, and 3. If the sample line was 8 inches long, the comparison lines on the right might be 6.25, 8, and 6.75 inches. One by one, each person will be asked which of the three lines on the right is the same length as the line on the left.

The researcher then leads your group through an example. It all appears to be very easy.

After the example, the researcher puts up a new set of cards. Each person gives an answer, the researcher writes it down, and the process is repeated until everyone has answered. Each time the person in the first chair answers first, the second chair answers second, and so on, until you, seated in the seventh chair, answer seventh. It's all very straightforward.

But after three rounds of this, something's not quite right. It looks like Line 2 matches the line on the left. But the person in the first chair says, "Line one." He says it crisply, firmly. He's wrong, obviously, but nobody seems to notice. No one glares at him. The researcher doesn't even react.

And then the person in the second chair says, "Line one." Again, no one flinches.

Without hesitation, the third person says, "Line one." And the fourth. And the fifth. And the sixth.

And now it's your turn. It's Line 2 that's the same length. Isn't it? But why did everybody else say Line 1? Is it some kind of illusion? Are you looking at this from a funny angle? Or maybe they are? Is it your eyes? Are they seeing more clearly than you? They all said Line 1. They couldn't all be wrong? Right?

You pause. You smile that uncomfortable, "I don't know what to do" smile. You hold your face in your hand for a moment. You look around. You furrow your brow. Is there an answer you're missing? Do you say what you think or what everybody else thinks? Are they going to be annoyed at you if you give a different answer? Is the researcher going to think you are the only one who can't do this right? Are you ruining the study?

And then, like three out of four people put in this exact situation, you sputter out: "Line one." You intentionally pick the wrong answer. You pick it because everybody else did. You refused what you saw in favor of what everybody said they saw.

And that is exactly what Solomon Asch wanted to know when he designed the study.[1] Would you state "a simple and clear matter of fact?" Or would you conform to the rest of the group and actually choose to be wrong?

What you didn't know was that everyone else in the group was told to give the same wrong answer. It was not a matter of perception or angles or eyesight. They were intentionally giving the wrong answer to see what you would do.

Asch built his study around a simple, definitive fact to underscore the scope of group conformity's power. Not only would we falter against a group's questionable opinions or arguably wrong assertions; we are stymied by a group united behind a demonstrably wrong basic fact.

That three out of four subjects in Asch's study gave in at least once to the group's wrong answer is illuminating. Just as striking are the comments Asch's subjects made when he asked them what was going through their minds as they gave wrong answers.

Many expressed pure deference to the group. "They must have been objectively correct if eight out of nine disagreed with me," one told Asch.

Others thought that the group was clearly wrong, but they lacked the confidence in themselves to stand firm. "I was sure they were wrong but not sure I was right," one subject said. Another said, "Either these guys were crazy or I was—I hadn't made up my mind which."

One of the most startling responses suggested that the subject thought the rest of the group was being tricked; he was disappointed in himself for not being tricked, too. "Perhaps it was an optical illusion which the others had grasped and I hadn't," he said, "At that point it seemed defective not to have the illusion they had."

Ultimately, these subjects wanted to fit in, even though the group was inherently temporary, the setting absurdly unnatural, and the others clearly wrong. They wanted this so desperately that they willed themselves to try to see what others saw. One subject told of the struggle he felt between wanting to be honest, wanting to seem smart, and wanting to fit in. "I like to be one of the boys, so to speak," he said, "so I was trying to see their lines as correct but succeeded only slightly, because there was always *my line*."

Ultimately it really didn't matter if subjects saw the group as right or wrong, because the group was more powerful than reality. As one person put it, "If they are wrong, then I'll be wrong, too."

What Asch showed is that adding people to the process made the obvious inaccessible. It made the simple painful. Alone, everyone would have identified the matching line and given the correct answer. In a group, the correct answer was sometimes elusive but almost always beside the point. What groups do best—as the leaders of prosthetic companies did for Katherine Bomkamp and as his assistants did for Robert Reich—is limit what you could otherwise clearly see.

Dan Scotto's job was to understand energy companies and advise his clients on whether to invest in them. As the head of his firm's research division, he had to find out everything he could about what these energy companies did and how well they did it. And then, just like an umpire who doesn't actually play but still affects the outcome of the game, he had to make the call. Clearly, definitively, he had to sum up his analysis with a recommendation to buy or avoid.

Dan did the fundamental analysis alone. He didn't have to worry that some larger team would feed him only the good news, as Robert Reich's assistants did, or that he would be rejected without a hearing, as Katherine Bomkamp was.

As he had done many hundreds of times before, in mid-August 2001 Dan gathered the stacks of financial information he needed to write a fresh piece of analysis on an energy company. What he saw was disconcerting. There was turmoil in the company's leadership. There were aborted acquisitions. There was softness in the core business divisions. But more than that, the balance sheet just didn't "pass the test." In short, there wasn't enough money coming into the company to sustain its debts and obligations. It was a problem made all the more pressing because this was "not a company with hard assets. It's built on paper and highly leveraged." In other words, when the company failed, and it would, it would go down fast.

Dan's report on Enron—headlined "All Stressed-up and No Place to Go"—was a warning to investors about a company then trading at more than $35 a share. That the company was built on layer upon layer of phony transactions was not known to Dan—or anyone outside the company and its accountants— but he had figured out that the fundamentals of the company did not add up and that trouble surely loomed.

Lest the underlying message of his soberly written report be missed by the investment community, Dan summarized his analysis in a follow-up conference call. Holdings in Enron, he said, "should be sold at all costs, and sold now."

A longtime Wall Street veteran, Dan was a highly respected analyst. In fact, the trade publication *Institutional Investor* had named him to their all-star team of analysts nine years running.

Three months after Dan's report, his analysis proved to be spot-on. Those Enron shares that were trading at $35 when Dan issued his warning were worthless. Investors who heeded Dan's advice saved thousands, or millions, or even billions. It was an example of the kind of foresight that can define a Wall Street career. Indeed, after three decades in the business, today

Dan mentions that report on Enron in the very first paragraph of his resume.

How did his employer react to the highlight of Dan's career? Three days after he circulated the report, his boss told him that he was barred from the office. They first put him on paid leave. He was told to go home, "cool off," and think about things. Later, his boss called and announced that the leave was over. And Dan was fired. Of Dan's Enron report, he said simply, "We don't think it was a good recommendation or a reasonable one."

The entire episode was a classic example of the capacity of a large group to make irrational decisions. "I looked at the numbers and I made a call based on what I saw," Dan said. "But when that report kicks around the company, there are investment bankers and higher-ups who are thinking about how Enron will never hire us, we'll never make fees from Enron with this thing out there."

To Dan, the essence of the Enron problem was that it had issued massive debt—generating great profits for investment banks and advisors—but the cupboards were bare. There were no assets to support additional debt, and the existing debt load was crushing.

Fixated on the problem of how to extract future revenue from Enron, Dan's company was oblivious to the reality that he had provided them a valuable solution. Not only was he going to save them the wasted effort of courting a bad company, he was providing them priceless investor credibility as the firm that warned the world about Enron.

"Instead, my bosses wanted to make more money from Enron in fees. Of course, that's fantasy," Dan said. "It's like trying to sell new deck chairs to the *Titanic*. I could see that, I could tell them that. But you get a dozen guys around a conference table, they're all looking at the little part they care about. And instead of an insightful warning, now my report looks like some kind of inciting garbage that's going to cost the company future business."

Not surprisingly, the experience encouraged Dan to move in a new direction. He opened his own small financial advising firm. His new firm does analysis and nothing else. "We don't have a division in charge of burying inconvenient research," Dan said. "We don't have a division in charge of acting contrary to what we know to be true. It's just straight analysis. Here's what we think, nothing more, nothing less."

LOOKING BACK, JORDAN will admit that the whole thing is kind of a setup. "How can you match those expectations?" she asks. "It is supposed to be the day you get to have all your dreams come true. Everything has to be perfect. *Everything.* You're Cinderella and here's your prince, and in this version, all your friends and family are perfect, too, and there is no wicked stepmother and the carriage doesn't turn into a pumpkin."

Unfortunately, Jordan and Aaron's wedding experience was anything but a fairy tale come true.

Jordan imagined something slightly modest but thoroughly charming. But very quickly she realized that it would hardly be up to her.

Aaron's parents invited Jordan's parents out for a friendly dinner to celebrate the engagement and talk about how his parents might help with the wedding planning. The gesture was not entirely welcome. Jordan's mother saw herself as the CEO of this wedding project, and now, before she'd even begun, there were these people butting in. Nevertheless, at Jordan's urging, her mother said they would welcome the help. Unexpectedly, Jordan's father even expressed an interest in all this, though Jordan suspected he was only concerned that the wedding not take place during football season.

Then Jordan's and Aaron's sisters chimed in as well. Surely they had a role here, too.

Forgotten in all this were Jordan and Aaron, the people getting married, who felt like they had to remind their self-appointed wedding committee that they were the reason any of this was happening.

That was, however, the only thing the group could agree on. Engagement parties. Bridal showers. Where, when, how many? What to do with the guests before the wedding? Welcome party? Luncheon? Golf? It was all up for debate.

As the events grew in scope, Jordan felt like the whole thing was slipping farther and farther away from her.

"This was supposed to be *my day*, but now it wasn't really mine and it wasn't all going to fit in a day," Jordan said.

There were bigger problems. Every little detail was battled over. Jordan's mother wanted a vintage look to the reception. It's classy, she said, and Jordan likes antiques. Aaron's sister made the case for a modern look. Jordan and Aaron both worked in technology, and she said that they should be celebrated in their own context.

The compromise made no one happy. The giant wedding cake looked like it had come from the not-too-distant future.

The centerpieces suggested that Benjamin Harrison might still be president.

Then there was the band. Jordan mentioned a local jazz combo she liked. Jordan's mother picked out a seven-member contemporary band. She said that they had more range, and that she wanted something more lively. Jordan said that jazz was the music of life. And on and on the battle of the bands raged, until they reached another unsatisfying compromise—they hired both.

It was the kind of schizophrenic group thinking that made investing in Enron seem like a good idea. Obsessed with the problem of making everything perfect, the wedding committee had made everything complicated. And now, instead of a Cinderella story, the wedding felt more like the revenge of the two-headed monster.

Worse than the feeling that the wedding was incoherent, there were the hurt feelings. Everyone involved felt as if there was something important that wasn't quite right because no one got their way.

Despite all the frustrations and urgent minor battles, it was a wonderful day for Jordan and Aaron. Nevertheless, Jordan has one word of advice for her friends when they get married: "Elope."

THE TAKEAWAY

When you have a big problem, you call for backup. We believe there is no problem we can't solve if we throw enough people at it.

But what does the second, or fifth, or tenth, or fiftieth person you bring in really add? They add incoherence, they add filters that keep information from you, and they add an even more powerful layer of fixation on the problem at hand that stands in the way of finding a solution.

Robert Reich, Dan Scotto, Katherine Bomkamp, and Jordan were all frustrated by the inherent weaknesses of group decision making. Dan and Katherine had to deal with a group's reflexive rejection of their ideas because the group couldn't see past the problems immediately in front of them. Robert Reich and Jordan had groups that wanted to make them happy, but addressing the problem of their happiness led to irrational decisions just the same.

When **75 percent of people will give an obviously wrong answer just to conform to a group's preference,** then there is no justification for the assumption that more people produce better answers.

Imagine you had twenty artists at your disposal. They would all paint a picture for you. Not twenty artists painting twenty different pictures, twenty artists painting one picture on the same canvas. You know what you would wind up with? No vision. Incoherence. Spoiled efforts as one artist's work spilled over and ruined what another was trying to do. In the end, you would have something less than what any single one of those artists could do by herself.

Two for the Road: Better Than a Group

Compete against yourself. You are working alone and up against a difficult task. You want multiple good ideas but you are only one person, with one perspective on things. A competition against yourself can help you nurture multiple idea streams and work from multiple vantage points.[2] You can pit your best idea from the morning against your best idea in the afternoon. The best idea at lunch versus the best idea in the office. As long as the context—time, place, something—is different, your thought process will be different, and you will be your own source of fresh perspective.

- - - - - - - -

Call your friend with purple hair. When we seek input from others, we have a tendency to listen to those most like ourselves. That means we listen to people who are most likely to see things as we see them, and who are least likely to offer a perspective that gets us around our problem. Sociologist Martin Ruef found that innovative business leaders tend to have a diverse array of friendships.[3] Those in business who are more conformist, and less successful, tend to spend their time surrounded by people just like themselves. You don't need an echo when you ask a question. Instead, talk to someone who sees everything differently.

CHAPTER 6

Four Points and the Wrongness of Always Being Right

WHAT IF YOU got lost driving? What trait would cause you the most trouble? It's not forgetfulness or exhaustion, it's confidence.

The confident lost person simply *knows* he will figure this whole thing out. He doesn't look for the source of the mistake, or pull over to get his bearings, or even think about asking for help. The confident lost person doesn't double back, he doubles down.

The confident lost person forges ahead and doesn't look back, because there's no time to waste. The sooner he executes his plan, the sooner he'll get there. He doesn't wonder why the landmark that's supposed to be on the left is on the right, or how he could be crossing the same bridge a second time. It's the confident lost person who keeps going the farthest down the wrong path.

We celebrate confidence as the natural by-product of our

ability and success. We treasure confidence as the resource that helps us do everything better. But we unleash confidence merely by doing something, anything, regardless of whether it's right or wrong. When confidence gets in the way of asking questions, then it no longer propels us forward, it chains us down.

DIANE RAVITCH IS an education policy expert who describes the modern American education reform movement and its test-first approach to schools as "like a freight train, and I'm out on the tracks saying, 'You're going the wrong way!'" What makes Ravitch's take on all this particularly interesting is that she used to be on that train, shouting, "Go faster."

As the Number 2 person in the United States Department of Education in the early 1990s, Ravitch helped lead a revolution. After many years as a researcher who studied and observed education policies, she was suddenly in a position to make policy. And she wasn't going to waste the opportunity shuffling around nickels and dimes. She wanted to advance an entirely new mind-set about how we think about schools, how we evaluate and reward them, how we challenge the top and elevate the bottom. In short, she wanted to figure out how to make schools do *everything better.* Even after leaving government, she stayed on the task to help see her reforms come to life. Ravitch was among the dominant voices at two leading education think tanks and helped run an organization that reviewed all the tests that were created out of the reforms she helped propagate.

Ravitch saw her work in clear terms. The problem was a

substandard education system that wasn't getting any better. The fix could be explained in one word: standards.

"Standards," she said, "are always a good thing. If we raised standards everywhere, then everyone would benefit. And when we do that, we dramatically reorient the bottom. For those at the bottom, more of the same would never be acceptable again."

There was a great hue and cry against the ideas Ravitch and her team were advancing. Experts and educators accused her of being narrow-minded, missing the breadth of what schools do and valuing only the smallest slice of a real education. Critics said she and her allies believed standards had an almost magical quality. If all you needed were high standards, they said, then every organization everywhere would get better just by raising its standards. That's nonsense, they asserted.

Ravitch had an answer for those critics. Stop hiding behind your words. Stop cowering behind your desks.

"Frankly, I thought they were afraid of tests," Ravitch said. Whether it was teachers, administrators, or policymakers, Ravitch thought "they were afraid that we would now hold what they were doing up to the light, and they would be exposed as failing our children."

Did she have doubts about her position? None. The correctness of her position was obvious. Everyone she knew told her she was right. "You're surrounded by people with the same ideas," Ravitch said. "You develop over the years a whole set of relationships with people who agree with you and congratulate you for what you're doing. There's not a lot of second-guessing going on in that circle."

Total confidence in her position was energizing. She went to work each day pressing ahead at full speed. She knew she was right. At least, she knew it until the day she didn't.

As Ravitch took a close look at the effects of the reforms she had fought for, she began to experience doubts. She imagined a new era of education built on incentives to teach more and teach better. What she saw was a new educational imperative based on one thing: teaching the test.

"We've created a system where Mrs. Smith is going to teach nothing but what's tested," Ravitch said.

The outcome is bitterly ironic to Ravitch. "In an effort to show how vitally important the classroom teacher is to learning, we undercut that teacher's ability to really teach," Ravitch said.

In fact, she thinks her movement traded away the most valuable classroom instruction in favor of a fundamentally useless skill. "We have reshaped the education system to an approach of 'right answers, right answers, right answers.' But life's not like that," she said. "We're putting a tremendous amount of value on being able to pick the right one out of four little bubbles. But this turns out not to be a very valuable skill. You can't take this skill out into the workplace and get paid for it."

It was a terribly painful process of conversion, but Ravitch saw no way around it. She had helped create a movement she now thinks is faddish, unsupported by evidence, and bad for our kids. The policy was fatally flawed and she had to start leading the fight against her own ideas.

Ravitch spent a good deal of time thinking about how she could have worked so hard pursuing the wrong policy. She realized that the researcher's skepticism that she normally applied was missing from her days as a policymaker.

"I was excited, caught up in the fervor of it," she said. "I always look for the hidden problems, the unstated assumptions, the unintended consequences in any idea. I reject nineteen out of twenty ideas that come across my desk as being half-baked. But I believed so strongly in myself and the people I was working with, I believed so strongly in the core idea, that I forgot to question it with the same skeptical eye."

Ravitch is on the outside now. She doesn't have the power to undo what she's done, only to question it. But she does stand together with a new set of allies—the very same people who were once her fiercest critics. "They have been wonderful to me, even those whose motives I once questioned," Ravitch said. "And the fact is, if I had been more open to considering their criticisms in the first place, I would have done a better job for our kids."

IN 1953, THE AVERAGE head coach of a major conference men's basketball team was paid about as much as one of those high school teachers Diane Ravitch worries about. Today, almost every head coach of a big conference team makes more than a million dollars per season, with several making large multiples of that.

That average coach in 1953 shouldered almost all of the tasks necessary to run a team. Unlike his modern-day successors, he didn't have four full-time assistant coaches, and a strength coach, and a nutritionist, and an academic coordinator.

Not surprisingly, coaches back then didn't typically see

themselves as hyperspecialized master technicians of the game, and the media offered little to feed and sustain outsized egos. Instead of the multibillion-dollar television contract in place now to broadcast every second of the NCAA Tournament, coaches in 1953 were competing to get to a championship game that wasn't even on national television.

An interesting thing has happened as college coaches have risen in stature over the last sixty years—teams have gotten worse at the most fundamental task of basketball! When the final buzzer sounded in a 2012 game between Georgetown and Tennessee, *neither team had made it to 40 points*. In a Mid-American Conference game in 2013, one team went into half-time having scored a total of four points. The bottom line: In 2013, men's college basketball teams scored fewer points per game than they did in 1953, or in any season in between.

How can that be? If you pay coaches more, if you put their work in the spotlight on television constantly, if you name the arenas and the courts after them, surely they will get better at their jobs?

Actually, what they will mainly see is how great and important they are. And great and important people must insert themselves in what's happening—all the time. In business schools they call it the *romance of leadership*. We see leaders as active. We see leaders as engaged. As leaders, the more active we are the more credit we can take. Diane Ravitch was a leader, so certain of herself that she believed her insistence on testing would be a panacea for our schools. College basketball coaches are leaders, so good at their jobs they must fix their teams all game long.

All this has pretty clear effects in college basketball today. Wally Szczerbiak, basketball analyst and a star of the 1999

NCAA Tournament, looks at college basketball today and sees "coaches smothering the game."

Instead of preparing their team and then watching them execute, coaches today actively insert themselves in the game as it happens. "They coach every single dribble," lamented Szczerbiak.

What happens next is entirely predictable. When you are being coached during a live game, you naturally do things more slowly. Listening, interpreting, and reacting take time and demand effort. It is harder to do what you're *being* told than to do what you've *been* taught. "There is no doubt about it," admits Brad Brownell, the head coach at Clemson University, "as coaches we slow them down."

Worse than that, while you are listening and interpreting, you are hampering your natural abilities, your honed instincts, and even your capacity to execute the lessons the coach spent several months of practice teaching. And then there is the hesitancy that comes with knowing every mistake is going to attract the coach's immediate wrath.

While overcoaching takes place throughout the game, it is particularly intense at the end of close games. "All those time-outs at the end of the game, all that talking instead of playing, that's fine for strategizing but it's terrible for doing," Szczerbiak said. "If you want me to shoot a basketball through a hoop, the last thing I want is for you to stop and sit me down for a few minutes and tell me to think about it. Basketball is a game of rhythm and feel. You don't get any rhythm sitting on your butt."

Teams scored more points—were better at playing basketball—with lower-stature coaches. American education,

Diane Ravitch believes, would be better today if she hadn't believed so fervently in herself. Supreme confidence is a tremendously powerful tool, but it's a tool that can attack the first available problem so relentlessly that no one has the perspective to consider if he or she is making the problem worse.

If Szczerbiak could call a timeout and gather all of today's coaches in a huddle, he would have a simple message. "In the history of the game, coaches have scored exactly zero points," he would tell them. "Remember that the next time you spend forty minutes exerting yourself on the sidelines trying to win the game. You want your team to score? Try sitting yourself down next time and letting the players play."

THERE's ALWAYS MORE information at your fingertips than you can possibly use. Do you want the quick-and-dirty count of starts and wins? Or do you like to look at the where, the when, the how fast, and against whom? Maybe just take the experts' view—what do they forecast? Or you could just straight play the odds.

There's a lot of ways to approach betting on a horse. But the basic transaction is the same. You make your pick. You step to the window and place your bet. And then you watch. In the span of a two-minute race, horses will grab positions on the inside and the outside, leads will be taken and surrendered, and your heart will thump as you await the outcome. Did your horse win or lose? Did *you* win or lose?

You're sitting in the grandstand, studying the horses in the sixth race. Now you've figured it out. You know which horse you want to bet on. On your way to the window you step over piles of discarded betting slips scattered over the floor. If you ever forgot that most bets are losers, you could just take a quick glance at the floor or listen to that little paper-crinkling sound that accompanies each step you take.

Just before you make it to the window, a fellow politely inquires if he could ask you just one quick question. You say fine. There's still plenty of time to place your bet before post time.

He says, "Would you look at this card and tell me the chance you think the horse you are going to bet on has of winning the race?"

The card has a number scale on it. It says one means you think your horse has a "slight" chance of winning. Seven means you think your horse has an "excellent" chance. The guy mentions not to worry about the odds or anything else, just say what *you* think your horse's chances are to win.

It turns out there is a second guy working the other end of the line, talking to people just after they place their bets. He asks the exact same question to a different group of bettors.

And what do you know, the people who get asked the question after they bet are 38 percent more confident of winning than the people asked before they bet.[1]

Their horses didn't get any faster. The odds didn't change. Nothing changed except one group was *about* to implement their decision and the other group had *already* implemented their decision.

The fancy term for this is post-decisional dissonance reduction. In simple terms, we generally have a lot of conflicting information available to us when we make a decision—any decision. We know there are reasons—some good reasons—why we should have done something differently. We tolerate all that conflict before we do something. But after we do it, we start tossing away the conflict. We start downgrading information that conflicts with what we did. We start elevating the importance of things that support our decision.

Betting on a horse race—like any decision—carries with it no end of data suggesting we should have done something else. There are reasons to support betting on other horses, or not betting at all. Before we bet, we acknowledge that conflict. After we bet, we cast conflict aside. I did the right thing. I'm confident I did.

This new confidence arrives so fast—in mere seconds—that we don't even have to think. We don't deliberate and rationally decide the only information that matters is supportive information. No, we give in to our instinct. Now that it's done, I'm sure I did the right thing. Otherwise, I wouldn't have done it.

One of the people interviewed before betting happened to bump into the other researcher talking to people who had already bet. He went up to him and said, "Are you working with that fellow there? Well, I just told him that my horse had a fair chance of winning. Will you have him change that to a good chance? No, by God, make that an excellent chance."

And that is post-decisional dissonance reduction. A minute had gone by. Nothing about the horse, the field, the track, the conditions had changed at all. But *the gambler* had changed in that minute. He went from someone about to act to someone who had acted. And now it was time to circle the wagons and support his action.

Because that's what we do. We increase the attractiveness

of what we've done and decrease the attractiveness of what we haven't done.

Unfortunately, our newfound confidence doesn't make us right. In fact, it makes it harder for us to succeed because we will have more trouble learning from our mistakes than we would if we realistically valued information before and after we acted.

It's that same ability to generate arbitrary confidence merely from doing that feeds college basketball coaches in their unshakable belief that interrupting the game to insert their wisdom is profitable even when scoring drops and drops. It's the same arbitrary confidence that let Diane Ravitch never question her education schemes while she was imposing them on classrooms across the nation. It's the same arbitrary confidence that fueled John Lennon's teachers as they wrote him off and the smoke jumpers as they went their own way. For bettors, for coaches, for Diane Ravitch, or for anyone, unquestioned confidence comes from doing something, no matter whether it was the right thing to do. In other words, when we're wrong, we're going to very happily keep being wrong.

THE PATIENTS INCLUDED the young and the old. There were men and women. Some were sick, others were injured.

But there were three things they all had in common. First, none had a condition that was even remotely life-threatening. Second, all suffered an inexplicable fatal or near-fatal episode while in the hospital. And third, all had come into contact with Dr. Michael Swango.

Today, Swango is serving consecutive life sentences after confessing to murdering several patients. The story of the serial-killing physician who poisoned patients in hospitals in the United States and abroad is chilling and inexplicable. But the pain he inflicted is all the more haunting because his superiors in his very first job could have stopped him—but their confidence in their profession got in the way.

After completing medical school, Swango was accepted into the residency program in surgery at Ohio State University. Inexplicably, Swango was chosen over scores of more qualified applicants. It took Swango an extra year to finish medical school because of concerns about his marginal performance, yet Ohio State accepted him over doctors who graduated on time, and with better grades from better schools.

In any case, from the outset Dr. Swango failed to live up to Ohio State's expectations. He was difficult to work with, sloppy, ill-prepared, and frequently cut corners on some of the pedestrian tasks required of a first-year resident, such as taking a patient's medical history. Midway through his first year, Ohio State's residency committee decided Dr. Swango would not be allowed to complete the multiyear program and that he would be dismissed at the end of the term.

Soon after Dr. Swango learned that he would be pushed out, there was a dramatic increase in the death rate in the hospital wing where he worked. An athletic nineteen-year-old woman inexplicably went into cardiac arrest and died. After several other deaths, there was a particularly eventful night when two sixty-year-old women suddenly suffered respiratory failure. Doctors descended on the patients, desperately trying to save their lives, and without the slightest idea what had caused their conditions. One of the women died; the other clung to life by the barest of margins.

Hospitals experience patient deaths regularly, of course. There is nothing remarkable or noteworthy about that. But the death rate jumped at Ohio State, and what would normally be a remarkably rare incidence of stable and strong patients inexplicably crashing turned commonplace. It would have been difficult to connect any of this to Dr. Michael Swango but for one small detail: There were witnesses.

The patient who survived the inexplicable respiratory arrest later told the doctors and nurses that just before the episode, a doctor matching Swango's description had come into her room with a syringe and injected it into her intravenous line.

There was a second witness. The patient in the next bed saw the exact same thing.

There was a third witness. A student nurse had entered the room and saw Dr. Swango, whom she identified by name, with the syringe.

Among the numerous alarming aspects of the witness reports is the fact that Dr. Swango had no medical reason to be in that hospital room, had no medical reason to ever be injecting something in the patient's IV tube, and would ultimately give conflicting answers regarding what he had been doing there, at one point claiming both that he was there to help a patient find her slippers and that he was never in the room.

Meanwhile, another nurse saw Dr. Swango leaving the bathroom of an unoccupied patient room. Thinking that a very odd sight—since doctors did not use patient bathrooms—she ducked her head into the bathroom. She found a syringe. Worried that the strange behavior indicated that Dr. Swango had done something wrong, she carefully wrapped the syringe and took it with her as evidence.

What did the doctors who ran the hospital do with this devastating and deadly turn of events? They closed ranks.

Though Dr. Swango's abilities were marginal and his work subpar, the hospital's leadership found it simply absurd to think that a physician, even one they were dismissing, was harming anyone. Quality, of course, is not related to confidence. It didn't take an extraordinary horse to inspire bettors' confidence, and it didn't even take an ordinary doctor to inspire the confidence of Ohio State's medical team.

Faced with inexplicable deaths, three witnesses, and a syringe, the doctors in charge decided that there was no reason to call the police. Instead, they launched their own, doctor-led investigation.

In short order they dismissed each witness's account. The patient who had nearly died could hardly be thought reliable given the trauma she had been through. Her roommate was labeled delusional. Surely the student nurse—for whom there was no convenient medical theory with which to dismiss her—must have been credible. Instead, the student nurse's testimony was considered simply mistaken. She was confused, that was all.

Was there poison in the syringe? Did it have Dr. Swango's fingerprints on it? Did it contain a substance ultimately found in the patient's bloodstream? Assuming it did not, the doctor-investigators never asked for it. They never had it tested. It sat packed safely away in the head nurse's desk for months, while she unsuccessfully sought someone, anyone in charge to examine it. Eventually she gave up hope that any doctor cared to find out the truth, and she threw it out.

The tragic consequences of the Keystone Cop-less investigation are abundantly clear. Dr. Swango simply walked away from Ohio State at the end of the term, only to find new positions first as a paramedic in Illinois, and then as a doctor in New York, South Dakota, and eventually overseas.

It would be sixteen years between the poisonings at Ohio State and Dr. Swango's murder convictions. In between, everywhere he went experienced inexplicable patient deaths.

It is, in short, a case of fatal overconfidence. The doctors at Ohio State believed so strongly in their profession, in themselves, and in the inherent superiority of their work and the people who performed it that they could not even fathom the threat Dr. Swango posed. They believed so much in themselves that the words of a student nurse, or even the head nurse, were just noise to them.

Rather than becoming increasingly concerned about a series of questionable actions and events, they gained confidence with each decision they made. They dismissed witnesses because they believed themselves to be right, dismissed evidence because they were right, dismissed the data that showed an extraordinary death rate because they were right. These doctors could not have done worse by their patients, by their hospital, and by their profession. And they couldn't have done any of it without extraordinary confidence that they knew what to do about the Dr. Swango problem.

When two filmmakers asked Kaleil Tuzman if they could make a documentary about the online business he was starting, he jumped at the opportunity.

The idea was entrancing to him. Not only would he wind up rich and successful when his company made it, but the whole thing would be captured on video. People would see what he had done. They would see the creativity, the drive. They would see the Kaleil charm. They would see the totality of his success. And it would never—never—be forgotten, because the film would live on forever.

Things didn't exactly work out that way.

Tuzman had been inspired by a long-forgotten parking ticket he found in the back of his closet. When he went online to find out if he needed to pay a late fee on top of the ticket fine, he couldn't get any information about it, much less actually pay the ticket. Kicking the idea around with a longtime buddy, they set out to create a company that would make it easier to connect local governments and people. Tuzman would run the financial side of the business and his longtime friend Tom Herman would run the technology side.

The company they started—ultimately named govWorks—was built around the image of the long lines people dread dealing with in dingy government offices. What if, they asked, we took an experience that the user hates and is expensive for the government to staff and replaced it with a transaction that was fast, painless, and cheap? What if, instead of waiting on line to pay a parking ticket, you could just click a button? What if, instead of waiting on line to file a building permit, you could just click a button?

The concept was very easy to explain. And it just made sense.

And Tuzman was nothing if not single-minded in pursuit of its success. He sold the promise of a company that could potentially extract a profit from $600 billion worth of government user transactions. It was a figure he touted day and night, in every meeting he had with potential investors. And the pitch worked. Tuzman secured more than $20 million in venture capital and $30 million in loans—more than enough to build a staff of hundreds who worked into the wee hours of the morning each day trying to build the product that would define the company and redefine government accessibility.

What Tuzman lacked was a sense of his own limits. Walking into one meeting with a major investment firm, he delivered a finely honed pitch about his company's business plan. Glaringly, though, what he lacked was even a basic understanding of what to do when the pitch proved successful. What portion of his company was he willing to cede in exchange for the biggest investment to date in govWorks? He didn't know. He was paralyzed by the investment firm's response—an offer that would immediately expire if he didn't accept the terms in full—because it hadn't occurred to him that there were two parts to such a meeting, his pitch and their response. And he wasn't ready for it.

Walking into another meeting with his cofounder by his side, Tuzman was stunned when Herman suggested a new feature for their website that they hadn't previously discussed. As Tuzman swatted away Herman's idea, it was clear that they had lost these investors. No one was going to put money in a company when the two principals couldn't agree on what the company did.

The gap in vision between Tuzman and Herman widened until ultimately Tuzman decided there was no longer room for both of them in the company. He fired his friend of more than a decade in a letter. Then he had security escort Herman from the building.

That he—like Diane Ravitch, and today's college basketball coaches, and the doctors at Ohio State, and all the horse bettors—displayed confidence unrelated to the quality of what he was doing was never more clear than when the company had to deliver an actual product. Despite attracting tens of millions of dollars in investments, and even securing the holy grail of parking ticket contracts—New York City—govWorks floundered on one simple measure. The software didn't work. Tuzman had spent all his time selling himself and his ability to create a visionary company. What he had not spent his time on was seeing to it that the company could actually do anything.

For Tuzman, there is no permanent record of his great success. When the credits rolled, all the money was gone, the company was sold for scrap and the stars of the documentary were Tuzman's ego and failure.

Nevertheless, the film makes clear that even those who lost money on Tuzman recognized that he could benefit from the experience. "I made a mistake with you," one investor told him. "I usually don't invest in people who haven't failed before."

Tuzman appreciates why many very successful investors respect failure. "It teaches you a lesson every single day," he said. "Personal invincibility is a great weapon until the day it fails, and then you learn it can make you spend an awful lot of energy on the wrong things."

The Takeaway

We believe in believing in ourselves. Nobody wants to cower timidly when something needs to be done. We step forward, confidently.

But just as trying harder and rounding up reinforcements can be both attractive and ineffective responses to a problem, so, too, is confidence a tool we are apt to pick up and misuse.

The problem with deploying confidence against a problem is that our confidence doesn't always come from our abilities and can distract us from potential solutions. Diane Ravitch's confidence helped her change education in America, and now she wishes it hadn't. College basketball coaches step confidently into the arena each night, yet that confidence helps many of them make an unproductive nuisance of themselves to their teams. Kaleil Tuzman's confidence helped him launch a company and the grandest of dreams—but got in the way of his noticing that the company's only product didn't work. "First, do no harm" is a fundamental principle taught to medical students. Yet the confidence of the doctors running the Ohio State University Hospital helped them allow irreparable harm. **We become 38 percent more confident about a decision merely because we can't undo it**. We can simply manufacture confidence, without regard to ability or reality.

Having vast confidence that you can fix a problem is like wearing eyeglasses you don't need. You will look at absolutely everything differently and see nothing clearly.

Two for the Road: Climbing out of the Overconfidence Trap

Make predictions. Think about one of your friends. If forced to choose between *The New Yorker* and *Vanity Fair*, which magazine would your friend subscribe to? How confident are you? How much would you bet that you are right? When psychologists asked people a series of these kinds of prediction questions, then asked the friends what they would really do, the predictions turned out to be spectacularly wrong—with 97 percent of the participants having been wildly overconfident that they were right. If they had been making real bets, participants would have lost almost every time.[2] Right now, make five predictions about something that could go either way. It could be anything. Which team is going to win the game tonight? Is it going to rain tomorrow? Anything. When you try to explain to yourself why one or two or all five of your predictions were wrong, remember there is no reason to pretend you are always right or that some outcomes aren't arbitrary. Even those capable of making the best predictions in the world don't know what will happen all the time—but they know better when they don't know.

- - - - - - - -

Shake It Up. How can you see something differently when you've already taught yourself how to "best" see things?

Shake it up, literally. In an experiment, researchers had some subjects move their arms in a fluid pattern, with big, sweeping movements.[3] Other subjects moved their arms in only short, precise patterns. Then, everyone took a creativity test, with questions covering such matters as how many uses you can think of for old newspapers. The fluid movers scored 24 percent higher on the creativity test. The body is a tangible metaphor for our thought process. In other words, a fluid, free-moving body produces new thoughts, while a rigid body is stuck with old answers.

CHAPTER 7

Miss Iceland, the Gangster, and the Cat: What Happens When You Burn the First Draft

IMAGINE YOU ARE on the television game show *Let's Make a Deal*.

The host offers you a choice: Would you like the prize behind door Number 1, door Number 2, or door Number 3? Behind two of the doors is a joke prize, like a goat. Behind one door is the grand prize, a new car.

You choose door Number 1. To make things more interesting, the host then opens door Number 3 and reveals a goat standing behind it. Now, he says, would you like to switch your pick to door Number 2, or stay with your first choice, door Number 1?

Our instinct, here and in so many other ways, is to stick with our first answer. We think of that first answer as the best answer. Otherwise, we wouldn't have given it in the first place.

Nevertheless, switching to door Number 2 would double your odds of winning.

It doesn't sound right. Shouldn't our chances be the same, at least? Our chances aren't the same, however, because the door that was opened wasn't chosen at random. It is never the door you picked and always a door with a goat that is opened.

This means that when you first chose a door, you had a one-third chance of being right. If you keep your original answer, your odds stay at one-third. But now, if you switch, with one of the goat doors eliminated for you, you raise that chance of winning to two-thirds. Your odds double because there was a two-thirds chance you chose a goat in the first place. Since the door for the car is never opened, switching now flips you from a two-thirds chance of a goat to a two-thirds chance of a car.

We have a first-answer bias. They are faster and easier, and it is intuitively pleasing to think that our first answer is our best answer. But it isn't.

How do we move problems out of the center of our thoughts? The first step is pushing past our first draft.

Pushing past a first draft lets you put the problem down. Pushing past the first draft is where you'll find the answer. The first draft of the *Jaws* script was obvious. Get yourself a giant shark. Have it eat people. It was the second draft—the one where Spielberg decided to make a shark movie without a shark—that didn't come from the pile of first available thoughts, and that made the movie a classic.

MOST PEOPLE THINK their jobs might be a little repetitious sometimes. But imagine coming in at the same time each day to say the very same words, and hear the very same responses.

That's been Catherine Russell's workday since Ronald Reagan was president, as she has played the same part in the same play for more than twenty-five years. The play flies so low under the radar that many theatergoers consider its existence an urban legend, according to the *New York Times*, which largely credits Russell (who also serves as general manager of the theater company) for its longevity. With eight performances a week, having never called in sick or taken a vacation, Catherine Russell has appeared in *Perfect Crime* more than 10,000 times. During a New York City transit strike, she drove around town picking up actors and crew members. During snowstorms and hurricanes she's found a way to the theater. The show must go on, after all. Russell's understudy surely has the least fulfilling job in the history of show business.

Russell has certainly made some history during her stint, including being officially recognized by *The Guinness Book of World Records* for having appeared in the same play more than anyone else has ever done. She's earned the nickname "the Cal Ripken of off-Broadway" and even had the chance to meet Cal Ripken himself. She takes a certain comfort in the belief that her record will never be broken—she figures there's no one who would be crazy enough to try.

If ever there was a person tempted to make do with first-draft thinking, it would be Catherine Russell. She hasn't even had to so much as learn a new line in more than twenty years since the playwright stopped tinkering with his creation and rewriting dialogue on the fly in the early years of its run.

Nevertheless, she challenges herself to bring something new to every performance as she constantly reinvents the part.

Perfect Crime is a murder mystery centered on Russell's character, Margaret, a psychiatrist who may have murdered her husband. Toward the end of the play, Margaret is interrogated by a police detective who hopes he might elicit a confession. Eager to disrupt the flow of the conversation, at one point Margaret blurts out "I love you" to the detective. The line could be taken for humor, for depravity, or even as a serious plot point. Should the audience laugh, gasp, or hang on the detective's response? Russell has explored all three possibilities. Indeed, she says, there are hundreds of ways to say "I love you," and "I've tried them all."

Initially the play was set to run for a month. The production had a good month and the run was extended. A few months later, the show committed to staying open for a year. Twenty-five years later, it is the longest-running play in New York theater history.

As much as she throws away the first draft in her acting, it was in her behind-the-scenes role that Catherine Russell ditched all initial impulses. Over its first seventeen years, the show had moved to various stages as leases expired and new venues were secured. In 2005, it appeared that the show would have to close. The company needed a new theater, and there was nothing available that fit the show's budget and needs. Staring straight at the problem would have meant the end of the line for the show and for Catherine Russell's role in it.

Hoping to keep a good thing going, Russell took charge. Understanding that there were no "theaters" available, she expanded the search. Was there a space available that they could turn into a theater? She found one in the form of a bankrupt beauty school. She formed a theater company to convert the beauty school into two theaters and a separate rehearsal space.

In keeping with her longevity theme, in the other theater Russell is running a new production of *The Fantasticks*. The original version ran for forty-two years and holds the record for the longest-running off-Broadway musical.

Meanwhile, the rehearsal space has been used by an array of acting luminaries, including Al Pacino.

As the general manager of the theater company, Catherine does more than star in the show every night. She oversees ticket sales and keeps an eye on the theater company's budget, and she's even had to fix a leaking toilet in the women's room. Most nights she solves problems until 7:50. Then she has ten minutes to get in character.

To keep the seats filled, she is constantly expanding the way the company sells tickets, using daily deals, social media, outreach to school groups, and other efforts. She takes great pride in the fact that her play's relatively low ticket prices mean that many first-time theatergoers come through the door.

For Russell, *Perfect Crime* has given her a career, and it's been a career of burning the first draft. Whose first draft would be to stay with a play, year after year after year? Whose first draft would be to continue redefining the role she played, and then to redefine it again? Whose first-draft response to learning there were no theaters available would be to create one on her own? In fact, it has been a life of second drafts, even as she's been reading from the same page the whole time.

In the end, there's a joy to the work and a surprising degree of variation for Catherine Russell. Every time the curtain rises, she's seen far past the problems right in front of her and found joy. As she tells acting students, loving your work is a triumph that must not be underestimated. "I say to them, 'When you're riding the subway in the morning, look around and see who looks happy to go to work. How many look happy?' They say, 'Not that many.' I say, 'If you want to be happy, you have to find work that you love to do.'"

A GOOD MAGAZINE article is like a chance encounter on a plane. For a brief moment it is at the center of your thoughts, but then it fades completely away.

Among the remarkable aspects of "Frank Sinatra Has a Cold," Gay Talese's 1966 Esquire magazine profile of Frank Sinatra, is that it is to this day remembered, discussed—revered, even. The story, with scenes, dialogue, action, and vivid descriptions, served as a clarion call to those who believed nonfiction could be as rich and gripping as fiction. It remains one of the original pillars of the New Journalism movement.

More than all that, it is still read because it is just plain interesting. With Sinatra dodging Talese's requests for an interview, Talese captures the man merely by circling in his orbit. Reading the profile, you genuinely feel that you have gained a glimpse into Sinatra's world, including those who enter and depart it in a flash.

Harlan Ellison was one such flash.

Ellison was just standing in the far corner of a club, watching some people playing pool.

Sinatra was there that night, sitting at the bar surrounded

by his team of yes-men and hangers-on. Sinatra noticed Ellison's boots. And he didn't like them.

From across the room, Sinatra starts in with Ellison about the boots. He tells him flatly, "I don't like the way you're dressed."

Then he asks Ellison what he does for a living. Ellison tells Sinatra that he is a plumber; another man in the club tells Sinatra that Ellison wrote a screenplay. With disdain, Sinatra dismisses it as a terrible movie. Ellison says it's not out yet.

It was just a banal distraction for Sinatra, who, as the title of the piece noted, was glumly fighting a cold. Talese aptly describes it as a moment that Sinatra probably forgot about three minutes later but that Harlan Ellison would remember for the rest of his life. But to the reader, Talese conveys the intensity of this ridiculously tiny moment and makes it come alive.

Like Catherine Russell's record-breaking run, the first great triumph of the Sinatra profile is merely that it exists. After giving Talese a noncommittal response, Sinatra's press agent ultimately refused to set up an interview for Talese. Anyone else would have been stymied by the thought of writing a profile of Frank Sinatra without Frank Sinatra. Talese himself at first thought that without an interview he wouldn't have much of a profile. But on second thought, he wondered if he could find something deeper and more interesting without the standard celebrity interview quotes.

Though he never did get to speak to Sinatra, Talese did speak to Harlan Ellison and a number of Sinatra's friends and acquaintances. More than that, he watched. He soaked in the atmosphere around a man who was once one of the biggest stars in the world but on the eve of his fiftieth birthday was facing a new reality. Neither he nor any singer of his day would ever again be the center of the music universe. That place had been assumed by Bob Dylan, the Beatles, and all the other new singer-songwriters who had taken over the industry. Not yet old enough to be a source of nostalgia, not young enough anymore to stake a new claim on success, Sinatra was, for the time, stuck. And Talese conveyed that feeling perfectly in confrontations over boots and other small moments.

Talese credits the depth and perspective of his writing to a process that is built to wring first-draft thinking out of his work. The elaborate steps he goes through offer him round after round after round of opportunity to reimagine his pieces and quash easy initial impulses.

He begins with elaborate notes. Oddly enough, for note taking he uses cardboard shirt inserts from his dry cleaners. From the material on his shirt inserts, he begins writing by hand on yellow legal pads. From the pads, he types his work out on a typewriter.

At each stage he is refining, reshaping, and recrafting his work.

When he has a first draft, he hardly imagines it as a finished or near-finished product. In fact, he takes his pages and pins them to the wall. Why? He is so committed to not assuming that the first draft should stand that he wants to "look at it fresh, as if somebody else wrote it."

At times he's even gone to the trouble of reading his pages at some distance—using binoculars and standing across the room—to maximize the feeling of looking at it new.

Even when he's reading his pages on a desk in front of him, he likes to make two copies. One copy is regular size. He shrinks the second copy to make it one-third smaller. He likes the effect of feeling like he is reading two different versions and giving each an independent read. "It helps me get a different perspective," Talese explained.

To Talese, a first draft of a story is just another set of notes. It has no standing to him. It is not nearly finished. It is just a step.

"I write and rewrite and rewrite and write," he said. And in throwing out first-draft thinking and pinning up the first draft itself for skeptical viewing, Talese transformed a forgettable Sinatra interview into an unforgettable piece that helped set a new standard for what nonfiction writing could be.

HERE'S A QUESTION you don't get asked every day. Imagine a distant planet. It's very different from Earth. Now, what do the creatures there look like? Think of one.

Take a moment. See it in your mind. Get something to write with. Draw one of these creatures. Right here in the margins. Draw it right now.

Okay, put your pencil down.

We have a very romantic notion of imagination. We think of imagination as both remarkably complex and inherently unique. We can't predict it, model it, contain it. The imagination is our own laboratory of infinite possibilities. Or so we hope.

But take a look at your creature. Did you give it eyes? How many? Two? Does it use those eyes for sight? Where did you put the eyes—are they above the mouth, or below? Are they placed symmetrically, or are they wildly uneven?

More likely than not, you gave your space alien eyes that work and look just like the eyes you know from humans and mammals and other familiar creatures. That's what the subjects in psychologist Thomas Ward's experiment did.[1] He asked them to dream up space creatures with any kind of shape, form, or function they chose, and they produced traditional Earth-like beings with familiar shapes, forms, and functions.

Ward's participants didn't sketch out creatures with wheels for feet or mouths on their legs. Their creatures generally did have legs, but they were just used for walking. Overall, 89 percent imagined a space being with no more than one major difference from Earth creatures.

Ward found that despite our capacity to access a virtually infinite imagination, our first take on an imaginative task is a product of tapping preestablished categories. Much the same way we know, reflexively, how to sort stacks of books or blocks into categories and subcategories, we tap existing categories as our first step in using our imagination—even when the task is to think of a creature that doesn't exist.

The category effect is so strong that when Ward conducted a second experiment—this time suggesting a category to his subjects—the results were as if his subjects had no imagination at all. In that second study, Ward again asked subjects to imagine a distant planet and a creature who lived there. This time, he told participants that the space creature had feathers. The alien creatures people drew came with wings, and beaks, and no ears—because the word *feathers* triggered the category *birds*, the subjects went no further in considering the question.

Here was an opportunity for a wild act of imagination— the subject's mind on a distant planet with who knows what kind of atmosphere and other conditions. Before them a blank sheet of paper and total freedom to conjure up something unique. And with just the mere hint of a category, we all wind up imagining a distant planet inhabited by giant ducks.

As Ward watched subjects give in to this categorization impulse, he wondered what would happen if you pushed people past their first category.

In his third experiment, Ward provided some background about his distant planet. The planet, he said, was almost entirely covered in molten lava. Between the vast oceans of lava, there were only a few islands of solid, inhabitable land. To survive, creatures on the planet needed to have the ability to travel from island to island in search of food.

To this he added one more detail. He told one group that the creatures of this planet had feathers. He told another group that the creatures of this planet had fur.

The feather group—given a terrain that demands flight and a creature with feathers—went about drawing up an array of pedestrian-looking birds.

But the fur group's instincts to immediately place this imaginative task within a simple categorization were thwarted. In effect, they were asked to think of something both birdlike and not birdlike. And the result was dramatic.

Instead of copying something familiar, people in this group created creatures that were entirely unique. Gone was the impulse that any creature with one bird feature should have every bird feature—thus the need to fly didn't mean the need for a beak or being without visible ears.

Lined up side by side, the work of the feather group is instantly recognizable as some variation on a common bird you could see in your backyard, while the work of the fur group looks like nothing you have ever seen.

The numbers show how profound a difference this made. In the feather group, even though they were imagining these birdlike beings living on a planet of molten lava, only 30 percent of the subjects gave their creature a novel, non-Earth feature to help them thrive in that environment. In the fur group, not only were they mixing features in a way not found here, but 57 percent gave their creature a unique adaptive ability not found on Earth.

The fur group had to push past their first-draft impulse to rely on what they already knew. Simply drawing a bird wouldn't work, because birds don't fit in the fur category. Pushing past that first draft doubled the fur group's core measure of creativity and eliminated the reflexive categorization that dictated the terms of the feather group's work.

As Ward's results illustrate, our first draft taps our first available category. Whatever problem we are trying to solve, our response is limited to things we already know, things that come to mind easily. Far from being impossible to predict, model, or contain, first-draft ideas are a reflex no more unique to you than the impulse to straighten your leg if you are hit right below the knee.

These first impulses block us from assembling unique combinations of knowledge or accessing truly original ideas. Instead, our first draft is a product of structured imagination. First drafts treat imagination challenges like a mathematics problem: We simply work from existing information, and we try to add it up.

Could Ward's subjects have come up with more creative

aliens? To Ward it is obvious: "The answer is yes. Subjects could have decided to pattern their creations after any of an infinite variety of visual forms, including recently encountered clouds, rocks, sand dunes, plates of spaghetti, or other entities." But they didn't if they stopped with their first draft.

Ward calls it "the path of least resistance and the tyranny of the particular." The fastest, easiest answer will be something you already know that comes to mind immediately and will not add anything new.

There is a better way. "Experiencing difficulty in developing a satisfactory product from a known exemplar can increase the possibility of creative outcomes," Ward notes. In plain English, if you are willing to throw away your first draft, you will create a better one—one that is vastly more innovative and useful.

ONE HUNDRED YEARS ago, the masters of the universe bought American railroads. "It was an institution, an image of man, a tradition, a code of honor, a source of poetry," Jacques Barzun wrote, but more than that, Wall Street tycoons and European barons were drawn to the industry by the promise of eternal wealth.

Fifty years later, the business was neither eternal nor profitable. Blue-chip railroads—the New York Central, the Pennsylvania Railroad—vanished under a mountain of debt. Others desperately sought mergers or bailouts or some kind of lifeline.

In 1960, when the *Harvard Business Review* took up the subject of the fall of the mighty American railroad, it said that the cause was myopia—that is, nearsightedness, lack of imagination, and absence of foresight. In other words, first-draft thinking.

The issue was that the railroad companies defined themselves around their product. They had the trains, the cars, the track. They were in the railroad business, and that had always been a great business to be in. But a customer who needs to move freight has no inherent need for trains. The ascendency of planes and trucks gave shippers an array of more flexible options—and they took advantage of them. In the process, railroad shipments declined despite a booming American economy and an explosion in the total quantity of goods shipped.

The *Harvard Business Review* describes the railroad tycoons of 1900 as "imperturbably self-confident." If you had told them then that in sixty years they would be "on their backs, broke, pleading for government subsidies, they would have thought you totally demented"—it was not possible, "not even a discussable subject or an askable question . . . the very thought was insane." Of course, they would have thought the jet airplane an insane proposition, too. By that measure, a lot of seemingly insane things come to be.

The railroads loved their first draft. The rail companies had built something great, and they intended to keep it just the way they had first imagined it. But as the *Harvard Business Review* warned, unless they shifted their focus from their product to their customer, they weren't going to be shipping anything at all.

Fifty years after the *Harvard Business Review* gave the railroad industry last rites, investment guru Warren Buffett made the single biggest acquisition of his career. It was what he called "an all-in bet." And what he went all-in on was an American railroad.

It was a stunning turn for an investor known for making big bets on the best-run companies. Some skeptics wondered if Buffett, known to have played with trains as a child, had finally slipped and let sentimentality instead of cold, hard numbers guide his decision making. Weren't there one hundred years of reasons not to buy railroads?

In announcing his purchase of the Burlington Northern Santa Fe Corporation, Buffett called it the kind of company that will be around for "two hundred years." He clearly enjoyed the fact that others had missed this opportunity because they didn't know what was happening in the railroad industry today.

No longer huddled together hoping to stall the passage of time, American railroads were now thriving, twenty-first-century companies. Railroads had, finally and decisively, thrown away the first draft.

Instead of assuming the value of rail, companies began integrating rail to best serve their customers' needs. Instead of ignoring other modes of transportation, railroads led the way on intermodal shipping, in which products can be seamlessly transferred from planes, trains, ships, and trucks all at one facility. Today, a portable cargo container might be snapped onto the back of a train car and moved within a few miles of its destination before being shifted to the back of a truck trailer for the final customer delivery.

Railroad companies also invested in better engines and more efficient designs, including double-stacking train cars. The result is that rail today is the unquestioned leader in moving freight at the lowest possible fuel cost. In terms of volume, one train can move the same amount of freight as 280 trucks.

Buffett pounced because he saw that the new American railroad company had figured out how to serve its customer. Like drawing truly original aliens after the right prompting, the railroads had finally thrown out the old categories, opened their minds, and moved on to the second draft. From the depths of 30 percent market share a half-century earlier, railroads today move more than half of all the freight in this country.

"It will be here," Buffett said without reservation. "A good railroad will be here as long as there is an American economy." That is, as long as they keep looking past the first draft.

AMERICA'S MOST WANTED aired sixteen segments focused on him. The FBI had a task force whose mission consisted entirely of finding him. Officials estimate that it was the most expensive manhunt in American law enforcement history. And yet, for eighteen years, convicted mob boss and murderer James "Whitey" Bulger eluded capture. No ordinary gangster, working in an industry not exactly known for its deportment, Bulger nevertheless stood out for being uniquely vicious and duplicitous.

Charlie Gasko had little in common with any infamous crime figure. Far from throwing money around, he seemed to have barely enough to live on. His clothes were plain. He didn't own a car or anything of value. His furniture was worn through. Charlie was known as a model tenant in his apartment complex. He was a man who never complained about anything or anyone, and of whom not an unkind word was uttered. Charlie was quiet, reclusive, quick to pet neighborhood strays, but otherwise entirely unremarkable.

Charlie liked to spend his time inside watching television. One show he never missed was *America's Most Wanted*. He probably saw all sixteen of those Whitey Bulger segments.

Despite their obvious differences, Charlie and Whitey did have one important thing in common—they were the same person. But the character Whitey had created was so unassuming that no one connected the two during thirteen years living in the same rent-controlled apartment in Santa Monica.

The FBI—unimaginatively using first-draft thinking—had sought Bulger by looking for a mob boss. "We were looking for a gangster and that was part of the problem," said Charles Fleming, a Boston police detective assigned to the FBI's Bulger task force. "He wasn't a gangster anymore."

While the FBI looked for mob boss Bulger living in luxury in Europe, the Charlie Gasko version barely left the house.

While the FBI tried to track Bulger's piles of money, Charlie Gasko lived like a senior citizen on a fixed income.

But with Osama bin Laden having recently been eliminated, Whitey Bulger became the FBI's most wanted man. Prompted by years of frustration and their target's newfound status, the FBI finally changed its approach to the search. As with the railroads, circumstances had finally shaken the FBI out of its commitment to the first draft and opened the path to the answer.

Instead of thinking about places a mob boss might live, they targeted places that might be agreeable for an eighty-year-old man. And instead of focusing on Bulger—not easily recognizable on the street, as years of experience and sixteen

America's Most Wanted profiles proved—they focused on Catherine Greig, Bulger's companion. Greig was more than twenty years younger than Bulger, and the FBI thought that at this stage she might leave a more distinctive and memorable impression with people.

With Greig as the focus, the FBI created a new television ad asking the public for help. It aired it in markets in California and elsewhere.

The ad hit the airwaves on a Monday. CNN did a story on the ads later that day. The CNN story was seen in Reykjavik, Iceland, by a former Miss Iceland who liked to spend her winters in Santa Monica.

She instantly recognized Catherine Greig because she had regularly seen Greig and Bulger feeding a stray cat on a nearby street corner and had sometimes stopped to chat with them.

Tuesday, the FBI received a call from Iceland.

Wednesday, with surveillance in place, the FBI confirmed that they had located Bulger and Greig. Bulger was duped into coming down to the apartment building's basement and arrested without incident. Greig then gave herself up.

Thus ended life on the run for one of the nation's most notorious crime figures. In the end he was undone not by violence or a flashy lifestyle but by the mundane habits of an ordinary old man who liked to pet stray cats. How did the FBI catch the gangster Whitey Bulger? They finally stopped focusing on the problem of the missing gangster and started looking for an old man.

The Takeaway

The first draft is the most obvious response to the problem at hand. It is the best way to define the situation on the problem's terms.

In the first draft, railroads didn't need to think about customers, the FBI looked for a gangster in gangster places, Catherine Russell gave up on the play that gave her a career, and Gay Talese canceled his profile of Frank Sinatra because Sinatra wouldn't talk to him.

But when you get past the first draft, you can see past the problem. The railroads redefined their business and again became the object of tycoon's dreams. The FBI redefined their search and got their man. Catherine Russell redefined her role and literally created her own stage. And Gay Talese redefined the forgettable celebrity profile and built a legacy on Sinatra not talking to him.

First drafts are unimaginative, built on the narrow categories provided by our problem. They are the first thing we can grab. As Thomas Ward found, **we are twice as creative when the first impulse doesn't work.**

A first draft is a magnifying glass, useful for taking a close look at what's right in front of you. Keep going past the first draft and you'll find a telescope, something that will help you see beyond what's closest and easiest to grab, and let you see what you've never seen before.

Two for the Road: Working on the Second Draft

Fail with joy. Try something that probably won't work. Try something that definitely won't work. We want to be right so much that we desperately try to cut out failing, but there's exploration and discovery to be found in failing. The cofounder of animation giant Pixar, Ed Catmull, describes their process as "going from suck to nonsuck." What they do is supposed to be bad in the beginning, and from the bad they create the magic. Andrew Stanton, director of Pixar hits *Finding Nemo* and *WALL-E*, says in filmmaking "my strategy has always been: Be wrong as fast as we can." Pixar's leaders understand that there is so much freedom and possibility in not being afraid to fail that failing first actually makes their movies better than if they had never failed at all.

— — — — — — — —

Do something out of order. Whatever your routine is, mix it up. Do things out of order. It can be as minor as putting your sandwich together backwards—put the jelly on first today and then the peanut butter. When researchers had people do mundane things out of order, they produced an 18 percent jump in cognitive flexibility scores that measure the capacity to build ideas from multiple concepts.[2]

CHAPTER 8

∷∷∷∷∷∷∷∷∷∷∷

The Knowledge Is Like a Toothache: The Value of Taking the Long Way

WHAT IF YOU needed to water some flowers on the far side of the yard? Would you grab the hose and go, or would you walk the whole distance first to clear a path so that the hose didn't get snagged on the way?

Most of us grab and go. And we *always* get snagged. The first, fastest, and most direct response is not the best or easiest solution.

When we have a problem we want an answer. We want it right now. We want it on schedule. But the answer is not going to come to you sitting at your desk when you summon it. It's not in the box marked "Answers." Your answer is on your pillow, it's in the park, it'll come to you while you are whistling to kill time waiting in line for lunch. The best answers are found when you put the problem down, give yourself time and space, change your context, and give your brain the opportunity to make connections and see what's possible.

Your best answer is not a pizza. It is not going to be delivered within thirty minutes. But it will come. And when it does, it will be more than you imagined you were capable of doing—and even better than pizza.

What should you do with the problem that's staring you in the face right now? Get up, physically get up from where you are stumped. Now, put down the problem. Think about something else, anything else. And give yourself some time. If you can look away now, it will lead to a lifetime of answers.

From the name, it sounds like the title of a new television quiz show. But more than any game show, it's excruciating and dramatic and brings grown men to their knees.

It's The Knowledge.

Pass the test and the prize is a coveted license to drive a taxi in London.

What is The Knowledge? It's everything a taxi driver is required to know—and a driver is required to know everything.

It begins with knowing every street within six miles of the center of London. *Every* street. Every main road, every side street, every one-way segment of a street. Every street that intersects with every other street, and in what order. There are, in the center of London, a mere 26,000 streets to contend with.

One more thing about London streets. There's no logic to them. There's no symmetrical grid of streets of like lengths and predictable intersections. And there is no sequential set of street names. There's no such thing as a self-evident relationship between streets, as there is in the case of Manhattan's Forty-second Street, which is forty blocks south of Eighty-second Street, and Fifth Avenue, which is three blocks east of Eighth Avenue. Instead, the streets of London are haphazardly named and crisscross each other like the contents of a bowl full of spaghetti dropped on the floor.

And then there are the landmarks. A driver is expected to know Big Ben, and Buckingham Palace, and the London Bridge—but also every museum, restaurant, hotel, hospital. It adds up to more than 186,000 locations. A driver needs to know what street these landmarks are on, and which side of the street, and then calculate the best way to get there from any starting point in the city.

The Knowledge test itself takes place in a small office, with a single test taker appearing before the examiner. The applicant wears dress clothes, addresses the examiner as "Sir," and must not be even a moment late.

The examiner enters, looking like a skeptical cop who doesn't quite believe your story. "You can smell if people have what is needed," said Alan Price, a veteran examiner.

The examiner proceeds to open his file and states a starting point and a destination. The prospective driver must then lay out the best route in perfect detail, narrating through each turn and every landmark on the way using only the map he's created in his head.

While the applicant sweats and strains against a mistake, the examiner sits imperiously waiting for an error, with an actual map at his side.

It is all so nerve-racking, "When a guy leaves this office, he won't even remember his own name," Price said.

Even so, the process is not over. Far from it. After successfully creating routes to four destinations selected by the examiner, the applicant is sent away. Come back in three or five or eight weeks, and answer another set of questions, he is told.

The process continues with session after session after session spread out over well more than a year. "The Knowledge is like a toothache," Price admitted. "It doesn't go away."

Why does it take so long to take the test?

Though it is a very strange system—and reportedly a 450-year-old relic from a time when even an English baron couldn't find someone who knew the streets of London—it is also a remarkably effective one.

Imagine the fate of a prospective driver who tried to learn all of London in one sitting. The problem would be overwhelming. Anyone would give up against the enormity of the task.

But street by street, day by day, it can be done.

And now we can even watch as the brain does it.

Researchers at University College London's Institute of Neurology were curious what driving a London taxi and preparing for The Knowledge does to a human brain. Cab drivers, many inclined to believe that they were a breed apart and richly deserving of a researcher's attention, gladly lined up to have their brains scanned.

With MRI scans taken throughout the process, researchers could see the hippocampus in drivers' brains grow as they studied to acquire The Knowledge and as they became more experienced drivers.

The hippocampus is the part of the brain that guides navigation. It is larger in birds and animals that depend upon keen navigation skills for survival. As these cab drivers built their mental map of the city, their brains grew to preserve those maps.

Interestingly, this doesn't happen for bus drivers, who drive through the same streets over and over again so have no need for a comprehensive map of the city in their heads. It doesn't happen for average residents of the city, who must nevertheless try to find their way across the city. It happens only for taxi drivers, who have both an urgency to learn and a built-in pacing mechanism.

London could not be learned overnight. Any driver who tried would immediately give up. But the time between test appearances makes it possible. The time between tests puts the brain to work on the task instead of allowing the brain to become overwhelmed.

As examiner Price explained, "The Knowledge is like a big jug of water and your brain is like a cup. You pour it in slowly so you don't lose it. The Knowledge never stops."

On the surface, The Knowledge is just a really, really hard geography test. But drivers tend to see it as something much grander, because you learn more than that. You learn what you are capable of if you don't stare straight at the problem.

It wasn't just that Linus Pauling made contributions to organic chemistry *and* inorganic chemistry *and* quantum mechanics *and* molecular biology *and* medicine. It was the way he saw intersections between these fields no one else saw and in the process forever redefined what we know.

His insights into the chemical bond that links atoms into molecules—molecules that are the basis of all physical matter—was a foundational finding that won him a 1954 Nobel Prize, and which has shaped our understanding of chemistry, biology, and physics for generations.

Applying his own findings, Pauling discovered the molecular basis of disease and ushered in a breakthrough in treatment of sickle-cell anemia and other conditions.

Meanwhile, eight years after he won the Nobel for chemistry, he was awarded the Nobel Peace Prize for his efforts to stop the spread of nuclear weapons. Pauling remains the only person to win two, unshared Nobel Prizes, and the only person to win the Peace Prize and a Nobel in a scientific field.

How, exactly, does one become a latter-day Renaissance man like Pauling?

Happily, Pauling loved to write and speak about the process of thinking big thoughts and finding big answers. First, he said, breakthroughs are not simply a matter of collecting the best minds and assuming that they will produce the best answers. In fact, in total seriousness he told audiences that there were at least two hundred thousand Americans smarter than him. Nevertheless, it was unlikely those two hundred thousand were going to change the face of chemistry, or biology, or would need to clear space on their mantel for the Nobels they would win.

Second, Pauling said, great scientific advances aren't like building the Great Wall of China, each day adding a tiny bit to what was there the day before. Instead, scientific advances come in big, swirling new directions that leave us seemingly going in circles before we burst forward with a new discovery.

Third, and most importantly, Pauling believed that working nonstop on any project limited the kind of insights he could arrive at. From one hour to the next, from one day to the next, he was likely to keep doing similar work and keep finding similar results. Doing this was like standing as a nightwatchman, guarding your ideas lest any new ones emerge. Which is why Pauling's advice to anyone trying to do something big amounted to three words: Put it down.

Pauling said he didn't do his best thinking in a laboratory, a classroom, the library, or during any great scientific meeting. It was in bed. It was away from the work and the details and the complications. In bed, as he drifted off to sleep, he set his mind free to try out new ideas and to seek new answers.

Working at the intersection of several fields, Pauling believed that he could combine ideas and principles in an infinite number of ways to seek a discovery. Most of those combinations— nearly all of them—were utterly useless. But Pauling believed that his mind, if unconstrained and unpressured, could sift and sort through those combinations without his active direction. And if something proved interesting, that idea would bubble up to conscious attention.

As Pauling extolled the virtue of letting the mind do its work, he hastened to tell students or anyone in his audience that the process of setting the mind free, of letting the imagination stretch to its capacity, was important for the scientist but just as vital "for the worker in any other field." For the poet, for the salesperson, for the car mechanic, a mind free to puzzle something over was sure to see past the limits placed on it when facing a problem directly.

For Pauling, it was this freedom to step away that continually took him past the problem he was working on and to the answer. Like the cab drivers who needed to give their minds time to grow, Pauling needed to give his mind the free time to grasp his next great idea.

You step into a small, plain room.

You see a chair, a table, and a bell.

You were told that this was the "surprise room," but so far it's not really living up to its name.

You are shown a box of toys and told you can play with those later. But first, would you like a treat?

You answer yes. Of course you would, because this study takes place when you're four years old.

The nice man you met in your preschool class explains that he's going to leave you alone for a few minutes. But if you want him to come back, all you have to do is ring the bell, and he will. You practice a couple of times. He goes out the door. You ring the bell. He comes right back. You do all that a second and then a third time.

Then the man reaches under the table and picks up a plate. He puts it on the table. There's a marshmallow on it.

The man says that if you can sit in the chair, and not get up, and wait until he comes back, then you can have *two* marshmallows.

Or, you can ring the bell anytime you want and he'll come right back. But if you ring the bell, you can only have *one* marshmallow.

The man explains the whole thing a second time.

Then he asks if you know what you will get if you wait. He asks how to get him to come back. He asks how many marshmallows you get if you ring the bell.

You answer his questions. He says that's right. And then he leaves.

He leaves you alone with that marshmallow.

What do you do?

You want to wait. Two marshmallows are better than one. But waiting is so hard. You want that marshmallow now. Right now.

There's the bell. Right in front of you. Ring it and the wait is over. Ring it and you can have a marshmallow.

Do you stare at the marshmallow? Does your mouth water? Are you thinking about how much fun it is to eat one? How tasty it will be?

Do you touch it? Poke it? Pick it up?

You can't go anywhere. You can't do anything. You can't even get out of your chair.

You could try to pass the time. Tap your feet. Or tug on your hair a bit. There's no one else to talk to, but you could talk to yourself. Maybe sing a little.

But the minutes tick by slowly. You're still in there. All alone. With the marshmallow. With the bell. You want to ring it. Waiting is no fun.

The force of the marshmallow proved to be too powerful for most kids. In fact, 70 percent of the four-year-olds who went through one of Walter Mischel's marshmallow experiments gave up waiting and gave up their chance for a second one.[1]

One of the many striking patterns Mischel uncovered in various versions of the marshmallow test is that the key to successfully waiting was being able to mentally put the marshmallow aside.

Staring at the marshmallow and longing to eat it was a

disastrous strategy. Singing the ABC song to yourself or pretending to be a cowboy, on the other hand, reduced the seductive power of that little ball of gelatinous goop.

Mischel saw this in his observations. The ones who gave up the fastest never took their focus off the marshmallow. The ones who lasted the longest "reduced their frustration during the delay period by selectively directing their attention and thoughts away from the rewards." In other words, they didn't focus on the problem.

He tested this conclusion by having the researcher give a new set of children one additional instruction before he left the room. To one group he provided transformational ideas. Think of that marshmallow as a cloud, or the moon. Think about playing in the clouds.

To the other group, the last thing the researcher said before stepping out the door was: Think about how marshmallows taste, how soft and sticky they are, how much fun they are to eat.

The average child in the cloud group lasted 13.5 minutes without ringing the bell. The typical child in the sticky and sweet group lasted 5.6 minutes.[2]

The sticky and sweet group was focused on the problem, and the problem quickly consumed them. The cloud group was given a way around thinking about the problem. They were given a break from it, and in the process they were freed of it.

That's the difference between paying close, relentless attention to a problem and casting your eyes away from the problem. An abstract focus leaves you patient and free, ready for a solution. An arousing, direct focus makes the problem overwhelming and unsolvable.

To function well, in the marshmallow test or in making any decision, we have to voluntarily postpone immediate gratification. It always feels better to pounce than to linger. But pouncing leaves us vulnerable. There's no way around the temptation of the marshmallow or the trap of the problem when we pounce.

Mischel thought that he had gleaned all he could from kids and marshmallows. But then he stumbled on a pattern that stunned him. Asking after the high school friends of his daughters, he came to think that many of these teenagers—who a decade earlier had been in the local preschool where he conducted his experiment—could be readily sorted based on how they had done on the marshmallow test. That is, those who waited for the second marshmallow seemed to be doing much better in school.

A full follow-up study confirmed his observation. The children who waited were more resilient, better able to handle stress, more self-assured, better at making plans and following through. They were, in short, still getting the outcomes they wanted and still displaying the patience and perseverance that guided them as preschoolers.

While many of the measures Mischel used were rather subjective, when he looked into his subjects' SAT scores he had the cold hard data that researchers crave. The difference between children who shortsightedly gave up and children who waited it out for the second marshmallow amounted to 210 points on the SAT. To put that into perspective, that is about the difference between being admitted to Yale University and being admitted to the State University of New York at Binghamton.

These patterns continued on as the preschoolers became adolescents and then adults. Those who had waited for the second marshmallow lived healthier lives as adults, were less likely to have a criminal record, had higher incomes, had greater feelings of self-worth, and were generally better able to cope with the challenges of life.[3]

For the marshmallow kids no less than Linus Pauling or the cab drivers, a bit of patience and the ability to look away moved them past the problem they were facing and let their minds work for them instead of against them.

VANESSA SELBST IS the most successful female player in poker history and among the most prominent and highly regarded players of either sex. When tennis great and poker enthusiast Rafael Nadal wanted to take on a top-level poker player, he squared off against Selbst. And she beat him. Handily.

She rose to the top of the game with a head for numbers and a fearlessness that's made her a master of sliding all her chips into the center of the table and betting her tournament life. It's a bet she likes to make even when her hand is weak.

Selbst developed both her passion for the game and her approach while she was a college student. Suddenly there was a deluge of poker on ESPN and other channels. And she was hooked.

Selbst was captivated by the fact that players came out of nowhere to win major tournaments—and millions of dollars.

And she was fascinated by the perspective into the game she could gain by watching. Watching on television, Selbst could see everyone's cards, while each player knew only his own. It gave her a window into the way players think individually and into the collective rhythm of it all. There was no other competition she had ever seen where the viewer could know so much more than the competitor about what's going on—and where the viewer could effectively train to beat that player just by watching.

There were, of course, countless hands where not much happened. One player had good cards and placed a big bet. The others had weak cards and quickly folded. But what interested Selbst was what happened when a player with weak cards tried to change the script. She saw a player storm back from barely holding onto his seat to become the chip leader on the strength of betting all he had on terrible cards. She watched his opponents—sitting with better cards and more chips—cower against him. They ran for the hills, and he collected the pot. After pulling this trick off three times, he had the chips and the swagger—and, soon enough, the tournament.

Selbst loved that poker was played at the intersection of math and psychology. You needed to know the odds of each scenario. How likely are you to get an ace here, or a club, or a pair. But more than that, you needed to understand human behavior. If you can figure out how others will react to what you do, you can dominate a game in which you can pretend to have anything at all.

Because more than what you actually have, poker is contested over the cards others think you have. Which to Selbst meant that the only way to win in poker was to be aggressive. "The aggressive player defines the hand," she said. "Everybody else is reacting and therefore vulnerable."

Reacting makes you vulnerable—not only because it allows the hand to progress on the aggressive player's terms but because it gives the aggressive player an easier read on what cards her opponent is most likely to have.

Even when Selbst finds an aggressive competitor in a game, she reasserts herself. When someone raises a bet against her—an aggressive move—she loves to reraise by several multiples more. "It makes people play a certain way against me. They don't want to reraise against me because they have no idea what I really have," she said. "That's a terrifying position to be in, and that's exactly what I want them to feel."

While she honed her strategy, Selbst continued to make relentless study of the competition and even of herself. She realized that in the heat of the moment, players make a default assumption that others will tend to react just as they do. Selbst saw this in herself as well.

"One of my leaks is thinking other players are as crazy as I am," she said. "Which means in a situation in which 95 percent of players would have a pair of aces but *I* would probably be bluffing, my first thought is the other guy is bluffing because that's what I would be doing."

Selbst has trained herself to overcome this reflexive reaction by taking just a slight pause when she's trying to read another player. She imagines getting up from her position and seeing things from the other player's seat. It's the patience to take that pause and look away from her cards—to stifle her own impulse and see something more—that makes the difference between an ordinary poker player and an extraordinary one. "You can't play like you are playing against yourself," she said. "Try to see it as someone else sees it, not as you see it.

Other people are terrible at this—which is a great advantage for me."

"It wasn't exactly anyone's idea of a happy, healthy childhood," Will readily admits.

Will and his sister Kim endured an angry, aggressive mother and a distant father who was out of the house most of the time and out of sight the rest.

"It just did not really matter what you did," Will said. "Either way, she was going to be on the attack. If you brought home good marks from school she would start right in with, 'So, you think you're better than me, huh?' But if you brought home bad marks, it would be, 'I always said you were a lazy bastard, never going to amount to much.'"

When Will and Kim were very young, they were stung and confused by the withering criticism and the total lack of physical affection. As they grew older, they tried to avoid their mother's attentions and just hoped to endure life at home until the day they could move out.

Embarrassment at how they lived led Will to try to keep his schoolmates at a distance. "I never wanted anyone to come over because I didn't want her to lay into me in front of somebody," he said. "I didn't want anyone to see that."

Through it all, at least, Will and Kim had each other. Each served as the other's sympathetic ear, shoulder to cry on, advocate, and coconspirator. "We survived together," he said. "I really thought we'd be close forever."

After they made it out, however, a distance opened up between them. "I guess we looked at each other and saw the past, what we had been through and what we were trying to escape," Will said.

They were polite, they were respectful, but Will and Kim treated each other more like work colleagues than treasured siblings.

It may have been uninspiring, but their adult relationship was functional for more than twenty years until they faced decisions about the long-term care of their father.

With their mother having passed away, their father rattled around for years in the family house. But he was losing his grip on independence. He needed help getting groceries and making meals and keeping the house up. He needed someone to keep his medications straight, and he needed prodding to remember to take them.

"We disagreed about what to do for him, and we disagreed about who would do what," Will said. "It was a stressful situation, and it didn't help that we were back in that house, feeling it all come back to us, caring for the man who had stood by and never done anything to make our lives tolerable for us. And now here we were turning our lives upside down to make life tolerable for him."

They didn't have the heart to take out a lifetime of resentment on him, though. And they couldn't take it out on their mother. So they chose the only target they could, each other.

They sniped at each other over schedules, unfinished chores, and even over whether they were being cheerful enough around their father.

Will moved something. Kim spent the day looking for it and then chewed him out about his thoughtlessness.

"And the pettiness just grew into something worse," he

said, "until we were screaming at each other like two drunks in a bar."

The irony of the situation was not lost on him. "We had to grow old before our time," Will said. "But now that we're adults, we're acting like children."

Things calmed to the point where they simply stopped speaking to each other. But the pain of the war against his sister wore on Will every day. "I thought back to all those times when we were little, huddled under the desk in her room while we waited out another one of Mom's storms," he said. "Kim was the one person in my life who would smile at me, hug me, encourage me. Now we couldn't even talk about the weather."

Will tried to find a way to make peace with Kim. Will's wife and Kim's husband were enlisted as go-betweens. But back and forth they went into their old house and their old pain, and out they came each time unable to see each other as they once did.

Nothing seemed to help, until an assignment at work forced Will to pull out of their shared caregiving schedule. He worried that his relationship with his sister would get even worse as he left her to deal with their father without his help.

Instead, the time apart initiated a healing process for the siblings.

Weeks later, Kim invited Will over to her house, where he had seldom been even before their fights began. She said to him, "If Mom could see us right now, she'd say, 'I was right about those two.'" She added, "I'm not going to let that happen." And with little more than a smile and a hug, there was an entirely different feeling between them.

As with the pause that helped Vanessa Selbst get a better

read on her opponents, Will and Kim emerged from time apart better able to see past the problem right in front of them.

"In the middle of it, we just couldn't stop being that way," Will said. "You can make something better if you just stop everything."

The Takeaway

Your brain—given time and space—can see past the problems that are right in front of you. It can heal wounded relationships, conquer opponents in poker, solve the mysteries of molecules. As any London cab driver can tell you, your brain—given time and space—can transform itself and let you conquer any test.

More than that, your brain can transform your life by letting you see past the marshmallow right in front of you to the things that lie beyond. **Children who looked away from the problem right in front of them went on to score 210 points higher on the SAT, and, what's more, they led better, easier lives as adults.**

Taking a step back from your problem and looking away—instead of pouncing on it—is like baking a cake instead of just eating each ingredient separately. It will take you longer, but you'll wind up with something much better in the end.

TWO FOR THE ROAD: SEEING FARTHER

"Learn to play the violin" was business guru Peter Drucker's memorable and surprising advice on how to best prepare to run a company. What he meant was that we need to be able to think across different subjects and nurture a larger vision. We need to be able to access more than one way of looking at something and take the time to add the pieces together. We need, in short, to cultivate seemingly unrelated strengths. Start learning something today that is totally unrelated to your work and family life, and it will teach you something vital about the things that are most important to you.

— — — — — — — —

Get out of your cubicle. Researchers put people in an actual box and asked them to perform some creative word tasks. Others did the exact same task outside the box.[4] The outside-the-boxers did 20 percent better. Get out of your confined space, be it cubicle, kitchen table, car, or wherever you are staring down a problem. Go where it is open—outside, in a big room, next to a giant window. Confinement confines ideas.

CHAPTER 9

Dark, Soft, Smooth, and Slow: The Power of Opposites

WHAT IF YOU wanted to build the best team in baseball? You would start with the best players, right?

If you assembled the highest-paid players in baseball for your team—those judged by general managers and owners to be the best in the game—you might be in for a surprise.

In 2013, three of the four highest-paid players in Major League Baseball were—to be blunt—worthless.

The three performed so modestly that the average minor leaguer could have done just as well—though those minor leaguers would cost only 1/63rd as much in salary.

Counterintuitively, if you wanted to be the best team, you would be far better off avoiding those commonly thought to be the best players.

When you are stumped by a problem—when the only thought you can abide is that this is a problem that cannot be solved—you have to open your mind to opposites. Flip the situation on its head. Consider the possibility that the obvious negative is really a positive. Within opposites we find our most creative selves.

IT WAS A hot day. A very hot day. At that time, air-conditioning was not yet a common feature in houses—and this particular California July day was scorching.

When his colleague arrived, the first thing Bob Wells told him was, "I am so hot today. I jumped in the pool, took a cold shower. I tried everything I could think of, and nothing worked."

Mel Tormé just nodded and sweated. The two men worked well at Wells's house in Toluca Lake, but Tormé thought that houses in the valley were 10 degrees warmer than everywhere else in southern California.

Wells handed Tormé a piece of paper and told him he had tried one more thing to cool off. "I sat down and wrote these few lines as an experiment," Wells said, "to see if thinking about winter scenes would do the job."

A Southern California winter being insufficiently cold, Wells imagined he was back in the East, living through a real New York City winter again.

Tormé looked at the sheet. On it he read, "Chestnuts roasting on an open fire, Jack Frost nipping at your nose, Yuletide carols being sung by a choir, and folks dressed up like Eskimos."

Wells apologetically said that the only winter thoughts he could keep in his head were of Christmas. The lines, he said, were just a throwaway, scribbled down for his own amusement in his failed attempt to beat the heat.

Tormé disagreed. He saw the makings of a song here. And since Tormé and Wells were under contract to produce new songs each month, they wasted no time following through.

Tormé sat down at the piano and began tinkering with some ideas. He tried out possible melody lines and chords. Meanwhile, Wells started building on the first verse.

As they sat there sweating in Wells's house, thinking about winter in July, within forty minutes they had "The Christmas Song."

They took it first to Nat King Cole. Tormé played the entire song for him, and Cole was ecstatic. He insisted that he be the first singer to record it. "That's my song," he told them. "Do you hear me? That is my song."

While their record company boss had initially dismissed it as a "one-day song," noting "No one is going to buy a song that's only good one day a year," Cole's enthusiasm won out.

Cole recorded it in 1946 and again in 1953 with the full orchestral backing that became the standard version we still know today. The song was a great hit for Cole, and for the songwriting team of Tormé and Wells. More than that, it has endured to become a holiday institution as the most recorded and most frequently played Christmas song ever.

How did they evoke the simple joy of the holiday? How did they create something that envelops you in such a specific feeling and transports you? Wells credits the lure of the song, and its resulting staying power, to the upside-down fact that they wrote it in July.

"If we wrote a Christmas song in December, there would be nothing memorable at all about it," he said. "We would have been surrounded by Christmas, by Christmas songs, by Christmas lines and Christmas hassles, and there would be nothing particularly magic in it. The moment would feel mundane to us and the song would be mundane."

Wells said that there is a difference between seeing something up close and seeing it straight on. "You don't write about a mountain from inside the mountain," he said. "If you did, you'd never get what people feel about it right."

Wells said that "the song is a true celebration of the Christmas season because that's what we felt when we wrote it" on that sweltering July day in Toluca Lake, when Christmas was just a dream to them.

DRUG USE IS a plague that can destroy people, families, communities, and even entire countries. What do you do about it?

You attack it with everything you have. It's a crime, so you bring in the police, make arrests, take the problem off the streets, and put those people in jail.

But the drug problem doesn't go away. It gets worse. What do you do?

Attack the problem harder. More police. More arrests. Longer prison sentences. All this is enormously expensive. It costs money and takes human effort. Today, every American state spends more on its jails than on its universities. When you have a clear enemy, you fight it with everything you have.

But what if the problem still doesn't go away? It only gets worse. Now what do you do? In most countries, the answer is obvious. Fight harder.

Not everybody saw things that way. "If what you are doing doesn't work, why keep doing it?" asks Dr. João Goulão, the head of antidrug efforts for the Portuguese government. Indeed, he noted that one highly cited definition of insanity is doing the same thing over and over and expecting different results.

Dr. Goulão and other government leaders opposed making an ever-increasing commitment to the tactics that were losing the battle. In fact, like Bob Wells and Mel Tormé seeing Christmas from a different light in July, Dr. Goulão and his colleagues wanted to wage their drug fight from the opposite direction.

Instead of more police and longer prison sentences, they proposed decriminalization of drug possession. "It's like we were banging our heads with a hammer to get rid of a headache," he said. "If that doesn't work, the answer isn't a bigger hammer."

Decriminalization! Critics howled. Drugs, already a scourge, would take over the country and make it uninhabitable. You don't take something wrong and essentially give it a government endorsement.

Dr. Goulão had an answer. Police and punishment—condemnation—these were never the goal. The goal—from the start—had always been reducing the use of drugs. If drug possession is decriminalized, he said, the country could put its resources into treatment. What's more, those in need of help would have no reason to hide in the shadows in fear of punishment if they sought a way out of drugs.

Ten years later, the drug numbers in Portugal are astonishing. Deaths from drug overdoses have fallen by 27 percent. New cases of HIV from drug use have fallen 71 percent. Overall drug use has fallen by 50 percent. Portugal now has the lowest rate of drug use in Europe. Portuguese people today are only one-fourth as likely to use drugs as Americans. "There is no doubt the phenomenon of addiction is in decline in Portugal," Dr. Goulão said, as every single researcher came to the same conclusion.

Dr. Goulão takes all this not as a personal triumph but as a triumph for the families affected. "It is impossible to overstate what this means for families in Portugal," he said. "Think of the mothers and fathers who are providing for their children today because they are not using, because they are not in jail. Our society is stronger today because of this."

Today, more than twenty nations have some form of drug decriminalization, though generally it is far more limited than Portugal's approach. Still, none of those countries has seen drug use go up in response to decriminalization.

Just as he once ignored his critics, today Dr. Goulão shrugs off those who praise him for having the courage and vision to turn drug policy on its head. "I am a doctor. Success to me is not how hard I work, or how many treatments I try on a patient, success to me is a healthy patient," he said. "If you look at drug use that way, the important thing isn't what you do, it's what happens. And what's happened is we have a healthier country now."

YOU'RE GOING TO be read a list of words. After each word, please respond with the next word that comes to mind.

It is important that you understand that there are no right or wrong answers. It is, however, essential that you respond each time with the very first word that comes to mind. Just say the word the moment it comes into your head. Again, there's no way to fail the test and no way to win on it, either. Just let your mind work without inhibition. Don't try to edit yourself.

And then the words start coming at you. What do you say?

"Dark."

"Soft."

"Smooth."

"Slow."

"Beautiful."

"High."

"Trouble."

"Hard."

"Justice."

"Light."

"Free."

"Bitter."

"Long."

"Joy."

"Quiet."

And on the list went for eighty-five more words.

Psychologists had been sorting through word association responses for generations, searching for insights into our personalities and proclivities. It wasn't until Albert Rothenberg developed his approach that anyone came up with a reliable way to use the test to gauge a person's capacity for creativity and finding answers.

Before Rothenberg, researchers counted up the number of unusual responses and theorized that odd word choices told us something about creativity. But unusual responses, it turned out, told us more about the size of a person's vocabulary than about the capacity to produce inventive answers.

Rothenberg developed a theory that creative responses are fed by the ability to conceive of contradictory concepts, ideas, and images. Holding opposing views at the same time gives a person the ability to see a situation from multiple angles. Those varied perspectives, then, dramatically increase the odds of identifying a unique or surprising solution.

In the case of word association, Rothenberg believed that the more often a respondent said a word directly opposite in meaning to the word read by the tester, the more likely it was that he or she was capable of creativity.

He tested this assumption by comparing the responses of people who regularly engaged in creative projects to those who did not. Rothenberg's assumptions were correct. The creative group replied with opposites 25 percent more often than the noncreative group—and gave the answers 12 percent faster.[1]

Rothenberg ran the test again and again, pairing off not just people who engaged in the creative arts but those who held creative leadership positions in business settings. Each time, the more creative group replied with a greater number of opposites.[2] He even collected responses from a dozen Nobel laureates—who turned out to give the greatest number of opposites in the shortest time of any group he ever tested.

In all these creative individuals, Rothenberg found that the speed of their responses when they replied with opposites was so great that these responses had to be summoned spontaneously. In other words, these subjects naturally classified a word with its opposites—holding two opposing notions right next to each other in their minds.

In interviews he conducted with novelists, poets, and other writers, Rothenberg was struck by the degree to which they held conflicting premises in the center of their thoughts. They worked with abstract and concrete ideas at the same time. They conceived of both the good and the bad within a person. They tolerated conflict, and it allowed them to find something new, something more. Indeed, Rothenberg found that it was by giving equal value to opposing beliefs that the writers were able to produce surprising and unique writing.

One of the fascinating elements of Rothenberg's results is that neither the use of opposites nor the degree of creativity a person demonstrates is related to intelligence. Rothenberg separately gave IQ tests to subjects who took the word association test—and IQ proved to have nothing to do with the use of opposites or the capacity to be creative. Similarly, when working with students, Rothenberg collected their SAT scores. Again, higher scores had no effect on creative capacity.

We often think creative solutions are the province of certain kinds of people. They are not. We can be creative, we can come up with the answer to anything, if we let ourselves. How many opposites did you use? If you had more than seven, you would have been in Rothenberg's creative group. Regardless of your number, you must keep your mind open to opposites. Open your mind to seeing past what is right in front of you, and answers will come.

When you have a problem, it plops down right in front of you. It's so easy to see that it almost demands we look at it. But if your mind is open to opposites, that means you can be simultaneously flummoxed by a problem and yet maintain the belief that the problem can be solved. You can see the problem right in front of you but also see around it to what's next. In fact,

Rothenberg found that the bigger the opposite concept you can accept, the bigger the creative, inventive thoughts you will produce. Or, put another way, the larger the problem you can ignore and the bigger the answer you can find.

When Paul Wellstone asked Bill Hillsman to make commercials for his U.S. Senate campaign, Wellstone had no money and no name recognition, and he was down more than 30 points in the polls. He was, in a word, hopeless.

But Hillsman, who loves a good challenge, jumped at the opportunity.

While other professionals in the campaign worked feverishly to overcome the money problem and make Wellstone appear more mainstream and senatorial, Hillsman saw things very differently.

Hillsman believed that political handlers were trapped in the same tired set of assumptions. They ran these paint-by-numbers campaigns in which they did the same things over and over again and failed miserably at identifying what was uniquely compelling about their candidate. As a result, the voters saw campaign ads on television and leapt for the mute button.

Hillsman saw something uniquely compelling in Wellstone— and it happened to be everything his handlers were trying to overcome. Like writing a Christmas song in July or fighting drugs by decriminalizing them, Hillsman saw the conventional approach to campaigns as flat, flawed, and boring. While the handlers tried to mold a generic Senate candidate out of a short, puffy-haired, emotional college professor, Hillsman thought that those weren't Wellstone's problems—they were his assets.

Hillsman didn't even worry about the dire money problem the campaign suffered. Instead of fruitlessly trying to close a 20-to-1 money gap with the opponent, Hillsman thought that the candidate should just make ads that were twenty times better than the opponents' ads. Instead of worrying that Wellstone didn't look like the candidate from central casting with perfect senatorial hair, Hillsman thought that they could present Wellstone as a real person, someone the voters could believe and like and trust.

With that frame of mind, and a willingness to ignore the rest of the campaign leadership, Hillsman started producing ads like no one had ever made before. He began with "Fast Paul," in which Wellstone talked fast and ran in and out of the frame as the background scene shifted from a hospital to a school to a riverbank. Wellstone started by saying he had to talk fast because he didn't have the millions of dollars his opponent had. In thirty seconds, he introduced his family, his background, and his top-issue priorities, and he defined the race as being run by a real person versus the big moneyed interest.

It wasn't the same ad voters had seen a million times from every candidate. No politician runs off the screen. No politician makes an ad touting how little money he has. No politician intentionally talks too fast. This was *different*. No need to hit the mute button on this—it was kind of fun and catchy. And you couldn't help absorb the message: This Wellstone guy is a real person.

Hillsman didn't ask the campaign to run tracking polls to

see whether the ad worked. They didn't have money for that, and Hillsman thought that he could get better data himself. He just went out to diners and ballgames and street corners and listened. If his ad is good enough, people will talk about it. If they don't talk about it, he's not doing his job right.

Hillsman followed up with an ad called "Looking for Rudy." It features Wellstone looking high and low in Minnesota for his opponent, the incumbent senator Rudy Boschwitz. Boschwitz had to that point refused to debate Wellstone and largely stayed in Washington, seeing Wellstone as no more than a minor nuisance who would be crushed on election day. Breaking all the rules of political advertising, Hillsman's ad was two minutes long instead of thirty seconds and contained not a single boilerplate talking point. Instead, unforgettably, it contained scenes like Wellstone dropping by Boschwitz's campaign headquarters and asking if the senator was there. He wasn't. Even better, Wellstone asks one staffer whether he thinks there should be a debate. The staffer looks stricken by the question and refuses to answer.

Later, Wellstone borrows a pen from the campaign receptionist to jot down his phone number to leave for Boschwitz. Noting that his campaign can't afford such nice pens, he asks if he can keep it.

Nobody was muting this. Nobody could even look away. Campaign ads were never this long, because who could possibly sit through two minutes of stock footage and overwritten tripe? But this—was compelling.

And on the ad goes, as Wellstone tries to track Rudy down at his business and tries in vain to get him on the phone.

The Wellstone campaign could afford to run the ad only one time. But it was so noteworthy that it was shown on local and national news programs, and it was so arresting that no one who saw it needed to see it again.

Paul Wellstone comes across as likable, affable, funny, and, most of all, a very real person. Boschwitz, in his absence, becomes this creature of Washington, too self-important to show up for the election.

"Looking for Rudy" was voted by one trade publication as the best political commercial ever made. In fact, the ad was so powerful that it embarrassed Boschwitz into agreeing to debate Wellstone. The debates amounted to more free advertising for a campaign without any money and helped Wellstone further the story line that he was a real person running against a Washington insider.

Hillsman is convinced that if the campaign had continued to treat the things that were different about Wellstone as problems, they would have lost by 40 points. Instead, the campaign was built around them, and when the votes were finally counted, Wellstone had risen from 40 points down to win the race by 47,000 votes.

Looking back on the race two decades later, Hillsman marvels at how little political advertising has advanced since then. "These ads are all research-driven, formulaic, and highly repetitive. There's very little art to them," he said. "All it does is telegraph that they're political commercials so people know right away to ignore it and go do something more worthwhile with the next thirty seconds of their life."

Hillsman thinks political ad makers behave as if they can somehow annoy people into voting for their candidate. If they tried to use these techniques in business, "they'd get thrown out the window."

The message of a typical political ad might as well be, "I'm just like all the rest of them," Hillsman said. If you want to stand out in the political ad business, on the other hand, "just do the opposite—highlight the things everyone else is afraid to show."

THE UNITED STATES had dedicated every available resource to its armed services in that winter of 1944. The nation was already churning out as many tanks and planes and weapons as it could. Soldiers were being inducted, trained, and sent overseas at an unheard-of rate. And still military leaders needed more help.

They were fighting two wars five thousand miles apart. They needed more soldiers; they needed more weapons. They always needed more.

But more was impossible. Everything that could be produced was being produced.

The only way to expand the American military capacity was to wait. But waiting was also impossible. The enemy would only grow stronger. Its appetite for conquest would only grow.

Stare at the problem and it has no answer. You need more. You can't have more. You will have to wait to get more. You can't wait. It's a loop from which there is no escape.

But flip the situation on its head—as the army did in 1944—and there is an answer. The point of an army isn't to be big and strong; the point is to win. Appearing big and strong will no doubt help you win, because the appearance of strength will intimidate an opponent and influence its behavior. So, army brass reasoned, even if you can't get more troops and tanks, it would be very useful to *appear* to have more troops and tanks.

With the formation of the 23rd Headquarters Special Troops, the army assembled a battalion of warriors who fought with their imaginations. Recruited from art schools and ad agencies, architecture firms and movie studios, their job was to conjure a fictional army battalion wherever it might be needed.

Troops in the 23rd fought in the war by not fighting at all—and they are credited with saving tens of thousands of lives by distracting and delaying enemy troops and keeping them from responding to real American attacks.

Men like the future fashion designer Bill Blass and future abstract impressionist painter Ellsworth Kelly and hundreds of other creative visionaries worked on what they called "atmosphere," creating a multifaceted impression of great military force that could be assembled as needed.

They designed inflatable versions of tanks, jeeps, and planes that could be deployed to trick German reconnaissance planes looking down from above.

They created the impression of a massive unit of advancing soldiers by appearing to send 100 transport trucks rumbling through the center of a French town—though actually it was two trucks driving through town, circling back around, and driving through again and again and again.

With sounds recorded at Fort Knox in Kentucky, they broadcast the roar of engines and the grinding of gears so that people for miles around would hear the approach of what seemed to be a massive force.

They acted out mini-plays in which troops from the 23rd would appear to drunkenly forget themselves for a moment and speak too loudly of the plans for the next attack while sitting in the corner of a French pub.

They created fake construction sites so that it appeared that they were just about to build a bridge, thus telegraphing a fictional battle route to the enemy.

In France, Luxembourg, Belgium, Holland, and Germany, the 23rd gave a constant series of false directions to the enemy.

Their last great mission helped the Americans cross the Rhine and begin the final phase of the defeat of Germany. With the real crossing planned for Remagen, the 23rd prepared to "attack" seventy-two miles downriver, in Viersen. The Viersen mission included thousands of inflatable tanks and jeeps, the full calliope of sound, fake bridge construction, and even a fake medical installation to prepare for the casualties of the fake attack.

One army general said that the Rhine diversion alone saved ten thousand lives.

The 23rd was a triumph of creativity—first in the creation of the team, and second in the freedom it allowed individual members to use the full force of their minds to fulfill the mission of looking strong.

Imagine responding to the fearsome German war machine with fake tanks and Bill Blass. It sounds like the opposite of the way to fight a war. It is—and that's why it worked so well.

THE TAKEAWAY

Being able to see the opposite opens up a world of new possibilities and original ideas. Seeing the opposite helped elect a senator on what others thought were his weaknesses. It helped win a war by playing pretend. It reduced the use of drugs by reducing the penalties for having them. It produced an iconic Christmas song on a sweltering summer day.

The power of tolerating the opposite is seeing things no one else can see, doing things that have never been done, believing when everyone else has given up. The limits people place on themselves no longer apply. Problems cannot stop you in your tracks if you can see the opposite—if you can see that problems can be gifts, as they were for Mel Tormé and Bob Wells and for Bill Hillsman. Seeing that problems can be challenges spurs innovative solutions—as in the Portuguese drug war and the American effort in World War II.

The power of turning things upside down is that it provides us the freedom to consider a new answer. That's why Arthur Rothenberg found that **creative people are 25 percent more focused on opposites.**

Turning a problem upside down is like opening the floodgates for your mind—you won't believe how much you had been holding back until you see the ideas that come rushing in.

Two for the Road: Go the Other Way

Don't follow the leader. We want to defer to the people in charge who have the knowledge and experience and judgment to arrive at the best answers. But the leader in many cases is just the person with bad ideas who has been

---

around the longest. When an economist examined NFL coaches' strategic decisions, he found that coaches failed to choose the more aggressive and beneficial option 89.8 percent of the time.[3] In academic-speak, coaches demonstrate "systematic, clear-cut, and . . . significant departures from the decisions that would maximize teams' chances of winning." In plain English, if the 32 top leaders in professional football are wrong 89.8 percent of the time, you should think past the well-worn answers of the people in charge.

— — — — — — — —

Digress. "Digression!" the boys in Holden Caulfield's class mockingly shout, when one of their classmates wanders off the central topic of his presentation. In one word, the scene in *Catcher in the Rye* encapsulates Holden's distress in a school that abhors unconventional thinking. Outside Holden's classroom, however, digressions should be treasured. When you bring together seemingly unrelated concepts, when you call in fugitive material, you see things in original ways and create original solutions. The next time you are trying to think of a bold answer, take the first opportunity to digress from the topic.

CHAPTER 10

- - - - - - - - - -

What Are These Bells For?
The Art of Listening to
Yourself

WHAT IF, BEFORE you told anyone else, you first had to test out all your ideas on a Magic 8 Ball? You would explain your plan, ask the ball if it was a good idea, shake the ball, and the ball would give any of a range of answers, including "Yes," "My reply is no," and "Ask again later."

We intuitively understand the absurdity of letting the Magic 8 Ball evaluate our thoughts and dash our hopes. But the reality is that the Magic 8 Ball would probably be a better sounding board than the next person you share an idea with. True, the Magic 8 Ball's responses are random, but at least it will never fall prey to the double-problem perspective.

Other people get caught in the morass of the problem you are facing. They get stuck in the details of the problem. Then, when you find a way to climb over the problem, other people look for a problem with your solution. The Magic 8 Ball, on the other hand, offers positive responses 50 percent of the time.

To give yourself a chance to find a solution, you must listen to your own voice. The solution is within you. But when you find the solution, the biggest threat you will face is letting someone else speak over your voice.

Other people will say no. Other people will share their doubts. It's not because you are wrong—it's because that's what other people do. They see the problem. If they could see a solution, they would have come up with one.

Unconstrained thought is power. It's your access to the answer. Every other voice is a harness that slows you down.

When it really matters, a single mind creates action, while a meeting of the minds creates hesitation and doubt.

Listen now.

You have the answer. The solution is within you. Listen to it.

How do you get people to do their very best work? Tell them what to do, show them, tell them again. Yell at them, remind them, restrict their options so that they have to do it the right way. Keep them at high alert. Pester them, insult them, do whatever is necessary to make clear what you want and make anything else unacceptable.

At least, that's how movies generally work. At the center of the bluster and buzz of activity is a director, barking out orders and tracking every detail to ensure that his vision comes to life.

How did Clint Eastwood direct Gene Hackman, Sean Penn, Tim Robbins, Morgan Freeman, and Hilary Swank to

Academy Award–winning performances? He did the opposite of all of those things.

Eastwood wants his actors to act, not to dangle on the end of a string he pulls. He wants his actors mentally engaged with the scene, not constantly drawn out by instructions and shouting and a sense of impending calamity. He believes the best work comes from talented individuals working to the very best of their ability, not from having one collective vision imposed on them.

Eastwood puts so much trust in his actors and their instincts that some initially question if they are up to the job. Tim Robbins, who won an Academy Award for his performance in Eastwood's *Mystic River*, said he initially felt intimidated by the freedom Eastwood provides actors to shape their performances. "You wonder if you can do it," Robbins said, "and then you find out very quickly, you can."

The process starts long before an actor steps onto the set. Eastwood doesn't want screen tests from his actors. He doesn't want to see how they would interpret the work when they know the least about the story and the character. He doesn't want them to feel trapped by their initial portrayal, or to think that they must replicate that for the film. Instead, he only looks at actors' previous work and thinks about what they would be capable of achieving in his films.

Eastwood's sets are calm. There are no bells ringing, no assistants running around shouting; no one snaps the clapper in an actor's face. No one is paid to interrupt and startle his actors and knock them out of their thoughts.

Eastwood had an inclination toward quiet sets, but it crystallized when he took a break from directing to star in *In the*

Line of Fire. "I walked on the set for *In the Line of Fire,* and there were bells going off," Eastwood explained. "There is a certain jarringness to the nerves when there's noise. And I said, 'What are these bells for? There isn't a fire.' And the assistant was yelling, and I said, 'Now just relax. If you're yelling, everyone is going to be yelling to get over your yelling. So just talk quietly and everybody will talk quietly along with you.'"

Because Eastwood believes that the best performances come from within, not without, he's quiet, too. He doesn't direct by watching the monitors; he watches the actors. And if he feels something, he's knows it's working. Instead of offering constant notes on the actors' performances, Eastwood doesn't have much to say at all. He doesn't offer his actors endless analysis of endless takes of each scene. In fact, he can't do that, because he doesn't do endless takes. Once or twice is enough for him.

The actors know that if they go for something emotionally draining, something just so, they need not worry about trying to robotically repeat the moment a dozen times. Actors thrive on the energy of knowing a great first take will be in the movie.

No one even shouts "Action!" on the set of an Eastwood movie, because no one would shout "Action!" in the lives of any of these characters. He wants his actors in the mind-set of their characters, not snapping into it like a machine. "I never could understand why the directors always had to yell, 'Action,'" Eastwood said. "It's kind of an adrenaline thing, but in certain scenes you don't want adrenaline."

Instead, Eastwood will start the cameras with a few quiet words—"Let's do this and see how it goes"—or with just a subtle roll of his finger. At times he films when the actors think they are just rehearsing, because he wants them to capture performances that feel freer, more natural and comfortable.

Most other directors shoot everything that happens in duplicate, with one camera recording film meant to be used in the final product and the other creating a disposable video for the director to watch on site to assess whether the scene worked. Eastwood, on the other hand, doesn't stop the production to watch the video and evaluate what he has. In fact, he doesn't even bother making the duplicate video copy. That means that when the scene is over he moves right on to the next one. The process feels more natural. And the actors don't have to constantly step out of character, because they'll be filming again shortly.

Eastwood's philosophy of directing comes down to a very simple premise: Do not get in the way. People will do their very best work when you let them. Morgan Freeman won an Academy Award when Eastwood directed him in *Million Dollar Baby*. He believes Eastwood's approach brought out his very best work, and that you could take what Eastwood does and apply it to running a business, a team, or life in general. "What Clint Eastwood learned long ago, and can teach the rest of us, is that people get off being left alone to do their jobs," Freeman said. "All he asks is that you come ready, just like him."

WARNED THAT THINGS were so bad in town that 50 percent of the children dropped out before finishing high school, Maurice Lim Miller's response caught his guide off guard. "Tell me about the other fifty percent," Miller said. "How do they make it through?"

And that is the essence of Miller's approach to battling poverty. In a social services universe built around what people can't do, Miller wants to understand what they can.

For many years Miller led an organization that worked very hard to lift people out of poverty with a traditional approach. They came into a family's life and they inserted themselves in everything. He vividly remembers the feeling when he accompanied one of his organization's social workers on a home visit. The family members were all newly arrived refugees who had fled genocide, navigated pirate-filled waters, and made their way to the other side of the world to begin new lives. And there the mother of the family stood, being lectured by a social worker half her age, told what she needed to do, where and when to do it. The mother submitted to the lecture, but across the room, her teenage son seethed with the indignity of it.

Miller understood the absurdity of the exchange. Here was his very well-meaning but sheltered social worker instructing a woman of boundless strength and fortitude on how to live her life. This was backwards. What, Miller wondered, could that woman teach us?

The social worker saw the woman as she had been trained to see her—as a case, as a problem, as someone defined by what she lacked. The woman didn't have the money necessary to provide for her family right now, and the social worker was there to address this problem.

But much as Clint Eastwood doubted the value of telling an actor how to act, Miller recoiled from telling poor people how to be poor.

Beyond his own organization, Miller came to believe that

almost every social service organization was set up around the same understanding of the poverty problem. "There is such a strong stereotype about the nation's poor—being low-income means being broken—that no one is interested [in] or even willing to consider and learn from low-income families," Miller said. In his experience, the policymakers, professionals, organizations, activists, and people who dole out grant money all see the world that way.

When Miller was a young boy, his mother struggled to keep food on the table. But asking for help was so demeaning that his mother simply couldn't bear it. Miller saw poverty through his mother's eyes, he saw it as that refugee family lived it, he saw it in every person assumed to be broken. He knew that when we give out help, we extract a price in pride, self-determination, and control. Getting help almost requires giving up. It requires adopting the same problem mind-set of the helpers. "The focus on need undermines our ability to see their strengths," Miller said of the way we respond to the poor. "And it undermines their ability to see their own strengths."

Miller wanted to break out of that mind-set. We need to take the blinders off, as he puts it. No more assumptions about what poor people lack. No more assumptions about the need for the poor to be told what to do.

Miller cast away the basic definition of the poor person problem, and it led him to an entirely new approach.

He started what he called the Family Independence Initiative with two dozen families in Oakland. He didn't hire any social workers, and he didn't tell these families what to do. Instead, *he asked*.

He asked the family members what they wanted to do with

their lives. He asked how they were going to reach their aspirations. He asked: What's the plan? What's next?

Breaking his families into three groups, he brought each group together as a ready-made social network of people who shared similar challenges and could look out for each other. He scheduled meetings for each group once a month and asked all involved to keep careful track of their goals and their efforts.

He had one firm rule for his staff. Never tell anyone what to do, and never tell anyone how to do it.

While the typical cost per family of a full-scale social service intervention was several times larger than Miller's budget, he believed that putting a computer in each household and offering no more than $200 a month in temporary assistance could help move these families toward their goals and ultimately have a transformative effect. "Poor people are not in free fall," Miller explained. "They don't need nets, they need springboards."

The effects were eye-opening. Family incomes jumped. People started savings accounts for the first time. Almost a third started some kind of business. The effects were not just financial. Miller's efforts all but eliminated the disastrous combination of desperation and isolation as the number of people in the program who said they had friends they could count on more than tripled over two years, to 91 percent.

The steps people in the program took may seem tiny, but the effects were monumental. Tamara, a single mother in San Francisco, had a steady job but faced a monthly struggle to pay the bills and the rent. When she joined the program she announced her goal: She wanted to be a city bus driver. Asked to lay out a concrete plan to reach her goal, she spelled out the steps that would get her to driving school and qualify her for driving a bus. The monthly meetings with other families gave her a sense of accountability, a need to show that she was serious and making progress.

She saved up enough to take a week off from her job to attend bus driving school. She aced the driving lessons and was a bus driver within weeks. The new salary was a security blanket. The fear that the money would run out before the month was over was gone. She started saving for a down payment on a house—and within two years she had moved her family into their first house.

Miller created the Family Independence Initiative because he didn't listen to what everyone else had to say about poverty. Now he asks the people he works with to do one thing: listen to themselves. "I didn't have the answer for Tamara's life," Miller happily admits. "She did."

IT'S SOME KIND of consumer preference study. They are going to ask you if you like some new kind of game or puzzle or something.

Pretty easy way to make a few dollars, and it won't take very long.

You are met at the door by a woman. She's a market researcher. She tells you she will be showing you some new products today and asking about your reaction.

As she leads you inside, you walk by an office with an open door. It's a plain room, with a desk, a chair, a filing cabinet, and a large bookcase piled high with stacks of files and papers.

She takes you to the conference room next door. You

now see it's actually part of the same room as that first office, separated by one of those accordion-style retractable room dividers.

The woman tells you that she has a questionnaire for you to fill out with questions on your interests and shopping habits. She says that while you fill out the form, she is going to do some work in her office. She will be back in ten minutes.

As you take a look at the questions, you hear her shuffling papers around on the other side of the accordion wall. You hear drawers open and close.

Four minutes later, though, it sounds as if the woman is moving something around in her office. If you listen closely, you hear her climb onto her chair. Apparently she's reaching for something on the top shelf of the bookcase.

And then the chair gives way. You hear a crash and a thud and a scream. The woman has fallen.

"Oh, my God, my foot . . . I . . . I . . . can't move it. Oh . . . my ankle," she cries.

"I . . . can't get this . . . thing . . . off me," the woman wails. The bookcase must have fallen on her.

She cries and moans.

What do you do?

Do you slide back the divider and see if you can help? Or walk around and go through the door?

Do you call out to her and ask if she needs help?

Do you just sit there and think about it, doing nothing to actually help?

This was, of course, the point of the experiment. There were no puzzles or games. There was only a carefully staged accident occurring just a few feet way. Did you help?

There was one key difference between those who got up to help and those who sat and did nothing. People who were alone when they filled out the questionnaire moved quickly to help the woman.[1] People who sat in the room with others filling out the survey at the same time usually did nothing at all. In fact, subjects who were alone were ten times more likely to help the woman than subjects who sat with others.

Why would there be such a huge difference? Everyone was hearing the same sounds of distress—the thumps and moans and cries were all coming from the same recording, so they were identical. Everyone was mere feet away from an injured woman. You didn't even have to get out of your chair to call out to her. You didn't even have to leave the room to peek behind the accordion wall. But if there was someone else there, that was too much to ask. Why?

As study authors Bibb Latané and Judith Rodin put it, "Bystanders look to others for guidance before acting."

With another person in the room, there was something else to factor in besides the needs of the injured woman—there was your standing relative to others. Are you doing the right thing? Are you overreacting? What does the other person think about what I'm doing? With another person there, we want our response validated.

When two or more people "overheard the emergency, they seemed noticeably confused and concerned, attempting to interpret what they heard and to decide on a course of action," Latané and Rodin wrote. "They often glanced furtively at one another, apparently anxious to discover the other's reaction yet unwilling to meet eyes and betray their own concern."

It's not that you don't care when you're in a group. But you want to care in the correct fashion.

When no one came to her aid, the researcher ultimately wriggled her way free and came limping through the door several minutes later. She asked people why they had not responded to her distress. No one said he or she was waiting to see what another person did. No one.

And that is the real power of group surrender. Not only do we place our ideas and our priorities behind others, but we surrender independence without even noticing we've put up the white flag.

When the woman came limping out, the subjects who had ignored her cries did not apologize. They did not take stock of themselves and swear to think for themselves from now on. The subjects couldn't see what they had done as being wrong, because they had obviously acted within boundaries the rest of the group found acceptable.

For the person sitting alone, however, there was no desperate hesitation. The same clear, internal voice that guides Clint Eastwood's actors and Maurice Lim Miller's participants guided them to act fast after the crash. That clear internal voice made them ready to help. It made them able to identify what needed to be done and do it. When we listen to our own voice, we are not trapped inside a problem wrapped inside another problem. When we listen to our own voice, we jump at the solution.

"There may be safety in numbers," Latané and Rodin concluded, "but these experiments suggest that if you are involved in an emergency, the best number of bystanders is one."

One bystander thinks and acts independently. One bystander genuinely responds. He doesn't gauge where he stands compared to others and measure their inclinations against his. One is the number for strong, decisive action, whether someone is trapped under a bookcase or needs to climb out of a dangerous and degrading life.

ONCE A WHORE, always a whore. The stinging words came out every time Miranda said she wanted to leave the life and go what they called "straight."

In fact, every time Miranda would tell one of the other prostitutes she knew that she needed to find something else to do with her life, she would hear the litany of reasons why it would never happen. She would never find a job that paid like this, if she was even lucky enough to ever find any job. She would never be able to fit into a button-down world anyway. And was she really going to be out there cutting the grass and painting the fence at the perfect little dream house she imagined living in?

When you boiled it all down, she couldn't stay in the life and she couldn't get out. Everyone else in the business saw the problem that was her life—and their lives, too—and told her just to accept it and give up, as they had.

As much as she couldn't stand the negativity from her peers, she had trouble figuring out how she could prove them wrong. She wondered what the first step to a regular life was. Quitting the life without something to do, without even a plan, seemed way too risky. But continuing to work while she figured things out was too depressing. She didn't know what to do to make what she needed to happen possible.

She did at least have her unusual hobby to lean on as a diversion. It was good for stress relief, a little humor, and even a little sense of triumph.

Miranda combined her professional expertise, her technological savvy, and a detective's eye for the detail that wasn't quite right into what she called her one-woman working girl's truth squad.

One by one, she had dedicated herself to revealing phonies, scams, and setups in the local prostitution industry. If something about a photo in an online ad didn't look quite right to her—maybe the lighting was just too good, or the angle of it suggested someone had really thought this through, or maybe the setting seemed too exotic and too far removed for a local girl—she labeled it a potential phony. Miranda then scoured the Internet looking for its source. Often the photo turned up in use by different prostitutes in different cities, all claiming to look just that good.

Miranda created her own online database of phony photos to warn her clients and anyone else that the woman in the photo wasn't really going to be there when they showed up. The fake photo was just meant to lure clients to the door—on the assumption that once they showed up they would have expended too much time and effort to up and leave at the sight of the actual, less attractive prostitute.

Miranda was also on the lookout for prostitutes who changed their working names. That smelled like a scam to her. She would try to link together the various names used by a woman, and then collect the comments made by her previous clients. Often the point of the name change was to bury a bad reputation for mistreating clients or stealing their money in a cash and dash scam. In its simplest form, a cash and dash prostitute would insist on being paid in full and in advance before heading inside to secure a hotel room. Instead of returning to the client with the room key, the prostitute leaves out the back door and is long gone before the client thinks to look for her. Variations include taking the money inside her apartment and then stepping into the bathroom to freshen up, only to have a frightening boyfriend type emerge from another room asking the man what he's doing there. Nobody ever gets their money back in these situations.

The other major red flag Miranda was on the lookout for was suspected police stings. When Miranda saw an ad for a new provider who insisted the client come to her but who was entirely vague about the experience and the price, she marked it as likely coming from Uncle Leo (that is, a law enforcement officer). The police could not get too far into the details—that would constitute entrapment. And they wanted to control the setting, so they insisted that clients come to them.

It was, she understood, a business of liars and cheats. But Miranda thought it didn't have to be. She believed every time someone was scammed, it just made it harder for her to keep the trust of a client and earn a living. And it was kind of fun picking out the phonies and shining her online spotlight on them.

It turned out that serving as kind of a Better Business Bureau for prostitution was doubly good for her business. Miranda wound up earning the loyalty of numerous clients—people she had saved from being scammed, stolen from, or arrested.

More than that, it turned out that it was her hobby that got her safely out of the business.

Enmeshed in a lengthy investigation of an escort agency website she suspected was fishy but that she couldn't quite pin down, Miranda turned to a message board favored by technology geeks and hackers. She described her interest in what she called "Internet sales scams" and asked for help cracking open a suspicious website.

Her question brought forth a flood of responses, including several that helped her see the coding underlying the site and figure out where it originated. After Miranda thanked the board for its help, one poster asked Miranda to contact him.

Nervous that one of these hackers had figured out her profession and was going to try to make life more difficult for her, Miranda nevertheless took a leap of faith and dashed off a quick message.

She was right. The poster did know what she did. But he was writing because he wanted to know if she was interested in a new line of work. The man ran an online reputation firm. Companies hired his company to make sure that their competitors were not manipulating reviews and trying to alter the market on phony grounds. Based on her keen eye for manipulation, the man thought Miranda might be a strong fit for his team.

He called her to discuss. The money was good. The hours were flexible. There was no rigid dress code. Miranda wanted to accept his offer before he'd finished making it. But then she caught herself. She asked for twenty-four hours to think it over. He said of course. She spent the time figuring out how the offer might be a scam.

But she couldn't find anything wrong with the man or the company. She quit her old job that day.

Miranda doesn't look back with scorn on the colleagues

who told her she'd never get out. They couldn't see what was possible for her—and there were many times she couldn't see it, either. "But I never stopped. I never thought that was all I could be," she said. "And it turned out I was right."

FOR JOE COULOMBE, there was one guiding principle he followed in starting his company and guiding it for almost three decades: Don't do what everybody else does.

Today, being different has brought his namesake store, Trader Joe's, a devoted following of shoppers who rave about the Greek yogurt and the pita crackers and the array of products that they can't get anywhere else. With Trader Joe's now in thirty-one states, fans who move to regions of the country without a store have even been known to launch massive petition drives pleading with the company to expand near them.

It's all enough to propel the company to more sales per square foot of store space than anyone else in the supermarket industry and a first-place ranking in consumer satisfaction. Trader Joe's profits are so reliable that, unlike its major competitors, it has no debt and keeps more than enough cash on hand to finance the construction of new locations.

It all started with a commitment to be different from the competition. When the supermarket industry was transforming from the modest-sized stores of the 1950s into the mega-stores common today, Trader Joe's was founded with stores one-fifth the size of a typical market. And it refuses to knock out walls to get bigger.

When he first started sketching out the Trader Joe's concept, friends in the industry told Coulombe that, in order to survive, he would need bigger stores, with more items. People want a store where they can get everything, they said. If you try to compete on the strength of a store that's about the size of two supermarket aisles, they warned him, you'll quickly be forgotten.

Coulombe believed he could work with what he had and make it an advantage. He would just make those two aisles unforgettable.

The size of his stores, though, was an accident of its legacy. Before Trader Joe's, Coulombe had run a group of Southern California convenience stores that were dying against intense competition.

For Coulombe, losing the stores would be like a Los Angeles Dodger striking out against a little league pitcher. He had an MBA from Stanford. He had been hired by his previous employer to learn everything there was to know about convenience stores. And after he helped that company launch its new convenience stores, he thought they were so promising he bought the stores himself. He was supposed to succeed beyond his imagining. And now, for all his credentials, he was failing at the simplest of businesses.

What could he possibly do to bring people to his stores? He didn't see an angle that would help him beat bigger chains with lower operating costs. But what would happen, he wondered, if he kept the convenience of his stores and the low prices but ditched all the chewing gum and potato chips and products people could buy everywhere and replaced all that with good stuff people couldn't get anywhere else?

He built the store around intriguing food items no one else had. When people found the wine or the sauce or the cracker or the cheese they loved, he hoped they would keep coming back for more. And because getting into and out of his stores was quick and easy, shoppers didn't mind that Joe didn't stock half the items on their grocery list.

Over the years, consultants told him again and again to fix that problem. They said he was limiting his own profits and missing an opportunity to expand beyond his niche because there were too many supermarket items Trader Joe's didn't carry. There was a limit to how far you could go on ten kinds of hummus and zero kinds of beer, they told him. But Joe understood, from his convenience store days, that if he offered what everybody else had, not many people would bother to come to his little store. "We adopted a policy of not carrying anything we could not be outstanding in," he said. If it didn't help differentiate his store, what was the point? In the process, Joe built a connection with customers that couldn't be shaken by the competition.

Joe built a unique connection with his store staff as well. Instead of following standard industry practice by paying near minimum wage and dividing the labor into rigidly specified tasks, he did the opposite. He set annual salaries at the median income of the store's region. He gave everyone who worked in the store the responsibility to serve the customer's needs first, so that whenever the checkout line backed up, every single employee was available to work the register or bag the groceries. It didn't take an MBA to see the return on this investment. Because they are well paid and engaged in the business, the staff is loyal to the company and turnover is lowest in the supermarket industry. Because they know the entire store and its products so well, the customer gets better service from a staff that can actually recommend products based on their personal experience.

There is also a little bit of adventure baked into a Trader Joe's visit. Despite the limited array of products, new items are continually introduced and certain existing items are phased out. Shoppers never know if they are going to stumble onto a new favorite when they come to the store. And the product buyers at Trader Joe's work to ensure that when they do offer something new, it's not the same trendy food item customers see everywhere but, instead, the next trend that hasn't happened yet.

"In that respect, we are not a conventional grocery store," Joe said. "We're closer to the fashion business than the supermarket business. And the reason we are so distinct is that when everyone told me I was wrong about this, I knew I must be onto something good."

The Takeaway

Clint Eastwood gets Oscar-winning performances out of his actors because he doesn't leave them worrying every minute about what he thinks. Maurice Lim Miller is transforming lives because he believes people have their own best answers. Trader Joe's is an industry leader and Miranda is living her dream because neither would listen when told to be just like all the rest.

The people around you can see your problem clearly, and, given the chance, they will see the problem in your answer. More importantly, if we are not careful, we'll let others do the thinking for us. **We are ten times more likely to help someone in distress when we are alone** because alone we can think for ourselves and see answers more clearly.

There's a reason your hometown is covered in Stop signs and not a single Go sign. Because go is natural. Go is automatic. Go is what we'd do all the time if we listened to our own voice. Stop is what other people say to us.

TWO FOR THE ROAD: TAKING
YOUR ANSWER FORWARD

Ignore the critic. Take the next criticism you get and ignore it. Don't worry about it. Don't answer it. Don't give it a thought. Larry Ellison, the CEO of computer services giant Oracle, warns that when you have a great, innovative idea, "you've got to be prepared for everyone telling you you're nuts." Indeed, Ellison said he cannot remember a single major decision he's made at the company that didn't draw fire from critics. "Sometimes people just throw labels at you and throw criticisms around that are not rational," he said. Instead, he ignores the doubters. "I let it go because you can't change behavior that you think is right just because someone is calling you names."

- - - - - - - -

Be mindful. Half the people in a University of Toronto study received lessons on mindfulness principles such as being slow to judge and being readily open to exploring new ideas. The other half did not. Then they all took what amounted to a distraction test, with unpleasant images periodically shown to see if they could be knocked off the task at hand. Those who had not had the mindfulness lesson wasted 276 percent more time on the useless, negative distraction photos.[2] Take a moment today to appreciate being open. Take a moment today to give yourself permission to see things differently. Take a moment today to be mindful, and you'll waste less time on what doesn't matter and open a clear path for your own ideas.

CONCLUSION

. . . .

What Do You Do
with Water?

EAST JAPAN RAILWAYS zoomed by its competitors with its superfast bullet train. Today it provides more than six billion passenger rides a year on the strength of its 199-mile-an-hour connections that can whisk a passenger from Tokyo to the other side of the country in a fraction of the time it takes to drive. In several regions the railway enjoys a market-share advantage of 99-to-1 over Japanese airlines.

The terrain of Japan has not made any of this easy for a railroad. In fact, the author of the classic book *100 Famous Japanese Mountains* had to leave more than a thousand Japanese mountains unmentioned.

For East Japan Railways, the fastest route between Japanese cities is through, not around or over, all these mountains. That means that the railroad had to become adept at building tunnels, and building them fast and cheap.

They had it all down to a basic routine when it was time to

drill a tunnel through Mt. Tanigawa, about 120 miles north-west of Tokyo.

Mt. Tanigawa, however, presented a new challenge. Its nickname alone—"the mountain of death"—should have been enough to give the railroad pause. Though not one of the world's tallest mountains, Tanigawa's combination of furious weather extremes and sharp inclines had reportedly claimed the lives of more rock climbers than any other mountain in the world.

East Japan Railways was not trying to climb the mountain, of course, just get through it. But they were stopped in their tracks, literally, when their tunnel through Mt. Tanigawa filled with water.

This was a problem.

The engineers on-site called for backup. What do we do? What do we do?

The best-paid minds in the company furrowed their brows and closely studied the situation. But when you start with a problem at the center of your thoughts, you don't consider the best possible answers—you fixate on the worst and most obvious obstacle. Water in the tunnel was the problem, so they drew up a plan to attack it.

They could not waterproof the tunnel. Water was still seeping in even as they tried that. There were really no alternatives, then, so they started drawing up plans for a drainage and aqueduct system to pump water out of the tunnel.

That was the plan. It was expensive and time-consuming. And yet, there wasn't a single engineer or manager in the company who had a better idea.

That is the essence of problem-based thinking. You define

everything on the problem's terms. You apply the tools the problem permits. You take the steps the problem suggests. You stay within the boundaries the problem provides. No matter how long you look at it, no matter how many more experts you bring in, it's still the same problem, with no alternatives but big losses and delays for the company.

What if you didn't start with the problem?

What if you didn't even think of the water *as* a problem?

Now, what do you do with water?

One of the mechanics who maintained the tunnel-digging equipment for the railroad wasn't worried about what to do with the water. That wasn't his job or his problem. In fact, he saw the water in an entirely different light. Thirsty one day, he bent down and took a large swallow of it. It was the best-tasting water he'd ever had. He took another swig and called his colleagues over. This stuff was good. It's so good we should bottle it.

The mechanic told his boss, who told his boss, who told the engineers, until the message had reached the top of the company. Thus was born Oshimizu water, a subsidiary of East Japan Railways.

It turned out that the water in the tunnel took a decades-long journey from the snowcap atop Mt. Tanigawa into the underground geologic strata. As it percolated up, it acquired an array of healthy minerals and the pure taste of nature.

The railway first sold the water from vending machines on its station platforms. But it proved so popular that they expanded production for home consumption. Ads tout the taste and purity of "the water from the snows of Mt. Tanigawa"—and consumers have responded by making the railway's water subsidiary a $75-million-a-year business.

Why did every single engineer miss this? They were trained to miss it. They were brought up to miss it. They were so wrapped up in seeing water as a problem that it never occurred to them that water in any other setting would be seen as an asset. Those engineers could have worked on the flooded Tanigawa tunnel for years—for the rest of their careers, probably—without imagining that the water itself was the solution to the water problem.

We tend to write ourselves off and think that only some small, select number of people can come up with extraordinary ideas. But you can solve anything if you refuse to view it as a problem—if you refuse to let the problem define your options.

Like those engineers, we've all been taught to work hard and attack problems head-on. That's common sense—and it's completely wrong. We have to recognize that our impulse to think problem-first is like putting on a set of handcuffs before we try to build something. It will make every single step harder—and ultimately limit what we can accomplish when responding to even the smallest problem.

None of those engineers wanted to waste the company's money—that's the opposite of what they wanted. But they were called in to fix a *problem*, they were trained in school to fix problems, so they rolled up their sleeves, and they did the very best they could within the limits the problem set for them.

Imagine casting off those limits. Imagine turning your biggest problem into an asset. You can.

Do not accept the problem's terms—and you will not only solve it—you'll be better off than when you started. You'll be better off for having had the problem. Nobody in East Japan Railways ever complains about all that water in the Tanigawa tunnel. They just drink it and count the profits.

ACKNOWLEDGMENTS

IT WOULD BE a rather weak endorsement for the premise of this book if I told you that writing it was just one big problem after another. Happily, that was not the case. In fact, writing it was great fun. Much of that is a credit to the wonderful people at St. Martin's Press who saw the power of this idea and helped me bring it to you. Nichole Argyres provided the three things authors most treasure in an editor: enthusiasm, insights, and patience. My thanks to the great work of the entire team from St. Martin's, including Laura Chasen, Karlyn Hixon, Laura Clark, and Allison Frascatore. Even before the first sentence was written, my agent, Sandy Choron, was excited about this book. My thanks to Sandy for her ardor and advocacy. Melinda Church's outlook, focus, and feedback helped me see how essential it was that I pursue this idea. Michael Bowen, Jared Port, Ben Leland, and Jordan Gentile listened with patience and good humor to tales of the writing process.

Sources

Introduction

Making of Jaws: *Jaws: The Inside Story*, Biography Channel (2009); Joseph McBride, *Steven Spielberg: A Biography*, Cambridge, MA: Da Capo Press (1999); and Steven Spielberg, interview by *Ain't It Cool News* (June 6, 2011).

Chapter 1

Ben Curtis: Bob Harig, "Ben Curtis' Title the Upset of All Upsets," ESPN.com (July 12, 2011); Doug Lesmerises, "Kent's Ben Curtis Enters Memorial Tournament with That Winning Feeling," *Cleveland Plain Dealer* (May 31, 2012); Paul Weber, "Golf: Victory Long Time Coming for Curtis," Associated Press (April 23, 2012).

Philip Schultz: Philip Schultz, "Words Failed, Then Saved Me," *New York Times* (September 3, 2011); Philip Schultz, *My Dyslexia*, New York: W. W. Norton & Company (2011); Philip Schultz, interview by *Talk of the Nation* (September 6, 2011).

Chapter 2

Seinfeld: Craig Tomasoff, "Programmers Keep Shows' Prospects in Focus (Groups)," *New York Times* (May 11, 2012); Andy Robin, "Innovation Story Studio," BusinessInnovationFactory.com (n.d.); "Forever

Seinfeld," *People* (May 14, 1998); Dennis Bjorklund, *Seinfeld Reference: The Complete Encyclopedia with Biographies, Character Profiles, and Episode Summaries,* Coralville, IA: Praetorian Publishing (2012); Rob Owen, "Test Audiences Still Have Sway in the Launch of a TV Series," *Pittsburgh Post-Gazette* (September 17, 2006); Ina Fried, "NBC's Zucker: 'Seinfeld' Wouldn't Make It Today," *CNET* (May 28, 2009); Jason Gots, "Seinfeld's Producer: Listen to Your Gut," *Big Think,* July 2, 2012; Ken Levine, "My Talk with Warren Littlefield," Kenlevine.blogspot.com (November 5, 2012).

Albert Einstein: Walter Isaacson, *Einstein: His Life and Universe,* New York: Simon & Schuster (2007); Ruth Moore, *Niels Bohr: The Man, His Science, and the World They Changed,* New York: Knopf (1966); Hans Ohanian, *Einstein's Mistakes: The Human Failings of Genius,* New York: W. W. Norton (2008); David Rowe and Robert Schulmann, *Einstein on Politics,* Princeton, NJ: Princeton University Press (2007).

CHAPTER 3

John Lennon: John Borack, *John Lennon: Life Is What Happens,* Iola, WI: Krause Publications (2010); Max Davidson, "A Poor School Report Is No Barrier to Success," *The Telegraph* (October 10, 2012); David Shelf, "Playboy Interview: John Lennon and Yoko Ono," *Playboy* (January 1981); Jacqueline Edmondson, *John Lennon: A Biography,* Westport, CT: Greenwood Press (2010); John Lennon, *In His Own Write,* New York: Simon & Schuster (1964); Claire Cohen, "Churchill? A Troublemaker. Lennon? A Useless Clown. And as for That Girl Thatcher . . . ," *The Daily Mail* (January 10, 2008); Barry Faulk, *British Rock Modernism, 1967–1977,* Burlington, VT: Ashgate Publishing (2010).

Coffee: P&G Sells Italian Coffee Unit. Press release (March 2, 1992); Rachel Larimore, "The Starbucks Guide to World Domination," *Slate* (October 24, 2013); Barton Weitz, "The Starbucks Coffee Company," Case study #36, University of Florida (2008); Mark Pendergrast, *Uncommon Grounds: The History of Coffee and How It Transformed the World,* New York: Basic Books (2010).

CHAPTER 4

Urban Meyer: Wright Thompson, "Urban Meyer Will Be Home for Dinner," *ESPN The Magazine* (August 22, 2012); Jodie Valade, "Urban Meyer Carries the Inspiration of His Father and a Mentor to Ohio State Football," *Cleveland Plain Dealer* (December 3, 2011); Pete Thamel, "For Coach of Unbeaten Utah, 'It Isn't Just About Football,'" *New York Times* (November 13, 2004).

Smokejumpers: Karl Weick, "The Collapse of Sensemaking in Organizations: The Mann Gulch Disaster," *Administrative Science Quarterly* 38 (1993): 628–52.

CHAPTER 5

Heated prosthetic: Nicole Laporte, "Don't Know How? Well, Find Someone Who Does," *New York Times* (November 26, 2011); Andrew Clay, "WVU Student Working to Help Veterans and Victims of Phantom Pain," WBOY.com (January 30, 2012); "WVU Student Inventor Taking London Stage," Associated Press (February 18. 2012); Joe Manchin, "Tribute to Katherine Bomkamp," *Congressional Record* (June 6, 2013).

Robert Reich: Robert Reich, *Locked in the Cabinet*, New York: Knopf (1997).

Enron: Rebecca Smith, "Ex-Analyst at BNP Paribas Warned His Clients in August About Enron," *Wall Street Journal* (January 29, 2002); Simon English, "Whistle-Blower Sent Off," *The Telegraph* (January 30, 2002); Shelter Chieza, "The Value of Reputation," *The Herald* (Zimbabwe) (May 22, 2013); David Larrabee and Jason Voss, *Valuation Techniques*, Hoboken, NJ: John Wiley & Sons (2013); Linda Tischler, "Jonathan Cohen: The Analyst," *Fast Company* (April 30, 2002).

CHAPTER 6

Diane Ravitch: Valerie Strauss, "The Diane Ravitch Myth," *Washington Post* (March 3, 2011); Kathryn Schulz, "Diane Ravitch on Being Wrong," *Slate* (May 17, 2010); Sam Dillon, "Scholar's School Reform U-Turn Shakes Up Debate," *New York Times* (March 2, 2010).

College Basketball: Adena Andrews, "Low Scoring the New Normal in College Basketball," CBSSports.com (February 25, 2013); Ray Glier, "In Men's Basketball, Scoring Suffers in Physical Game," *New York Times* (February 23, 2013).

Michael Swango: James Stewart, *Blind Eye: The Terrifying Story of a Doctor Who Got Away with Murder*, New York: Simon & Schuster (2000); Brent Larkin, "Ohio State University Can't Look the Other Way Forever When Bad News Breaks," *Cleveland Plain Dealer* (October 26, 2013); Ray Lockwood, "Swango to Be Tried for OSU Murders," *The Lantern* (October 16, 2000); "Ex-Doctor to Plead Guilty in Death," Associated Press (September 22, 2000); "How Dr. Michael Swango Became a Poisoner and Outwitted Two Medical Schools," *Cleveland Plain Dealer* (December 19, 1993).

Kaleil Tuzman: *Startup.com*, directed by Chris Hegedus and Jehane Noujaim, Artisan Entertainment (2001); Christopher Steiner, "Startup.com: The Sequel," *Forbes* (October 25, 2010); Rolfe Winkler, "Investors Need a First Aid KIT," *Wall Street Journal* (May 2, 2012); Dan Nakaso, "Dot-com Survior to Share with Hawaii His Lessons Learned," *Honolulu Advertiser* (April 18, 2002).

CHAPTER 7

Catherine Russell: Catherine Russell, "One Role, with 10,000 Variations," *New York Times* (October 29, 2011); Simi Horowitz, "Catherine Russell Hits 25 Years in Warren Manzi's 'Perfect Crime,'" *Backstage* (April 17, 2012); Aaron Carter, "Behold: Catherine Russell the Off-Broadway Force," Associated Press (March 7, 2013); Daniel Lehman, "Catherine Russell Celebrates 22 Years and 9,000 Performances in 'Perfect Crime,'" *Backstage* (April 16, 2009); Jason Zinoman, "Still Kicking After 18 Years of Homicide," *New York Times* (October 3, 2005).

Gay Talese: Ryan Kohls, "Gay Talese," *Whatiwannaknow.com* (March 3, 2012); Barbara Lounsberry, "Gay Talese and the Fine Art of Hanging Out," *Creative Nonfiction* 16 (2001); Gay Talese, *The*

Gay Talese Reader, New York: Walker Publishing (2003); Robert Boynton, *The New New Journalism: Conversations with America's Best Nonfiction Writers on Their Craft*, New York: Vintage (2005); Katie Roiphe, "Gay Talese, The Art of Nonfiction," *Paris Review* (Summer 2009).

Railroads: Theodore Levitt, "Marketing Myopia," *Harvard Business Review* (July–August 1960); "What Business Are You In? Classic Advice from Theodore Levitt," *Harvard Business Review* (October 2006); Greg Morcroft and Alistair Barr, "Berkshire Hathaway to Buy Burlington Northern Sante Fe," *MarketWatch* (November 3, 2009); Mary Buffett, "Why Warren Buffett Believes Trains Will Power the Recovery," *Huffington Post* (March 27, 2013); Warren Buffett, interview by Charlie Rose, *PBS* (November 13, 2009).

Whitey Bulger: Dick Lehr and Gerard O'Neill, *Whitey: The Life of America's Most Notorious Mob Boss*, New York: Crown Publishing (2013); Ted Mann, "Whitey Bulger's Downfall," *The Wire* (October 10, 2011); Shelley Murphy and Maria Cramer, "Whitey in Exile," *Boston Globe* (October 9, 2011).

CHAPTER 8

The Knowledge: "Taxi Drivers' Brains 'Grow' on the Job," *BBC News* (March 14, 2000); Ed Yong, "How Acquiring the Knowledge Changes the Brains of London Cab Drivers," *Discover* (December 8, 2011); Ferris Jabr, "Cache Cab: Taxi Drivers' Brains Grow to Navigate London's Streets," *Scientific American* (December 8, 2011); Andrew Anthony, "Where to, Guv'nor?" *The Guardian* (March 10, 2001); Eric Spitznagel, "Interview with a London Cabbie," *New York Times Magazine* (January 3, 2012).

Linus Pauling: Linus Pauling, *Linus Pauling in His Own Words*, New York: Simon & Schuster (1995).

Vanessa Selbst: Nick Pryce, "Laying Down the Law," *Poker Player* (July 2, 2013); Tim Struby, "Her Poker Face," *ESPN The Magazine* (June 27, 2013).

CHAPTER 9

The Christmas Song: Dale Nobbman, *Christmas Music Companion Fact Book*, Anaheim: Centerstream Publications (2000); Andrew Dansby, "'The Christmas Song' Was Born on a Very Hot Day," *Houston Chronicle* (December 7, 2012); Philip Furia and Michael Lasser, *America's Songs*, New York: Routledge (2006); Vance Garnett, "Four Famous Singers + Two Songs = A Very Merry Christmas," *Washington Times* (December 14, 2011).

Portugal's Drug Policy: Brian Vastag, "Five Years After: Portugal's Drug Decriminalization Policy Shows Positive Results," *Scientific American* (April 7, 2009); Samuel Blackstone, "Portugal Decriminalized All Drugs Eleven Years Ago and the Results Are Staggering," *Business Insider* (July 17, 2012); Maia Szalavitz, "Drugs in Portugal: Did Decriminalization Work?" *Time* (April 26, 2009); Coletta Youngers and John Walsh, "Drug Decriminalization: A Trend Takes Shape," *Americas Quarterly* (Fall 2009).

Bill Hillsman: Kevin Featherly, "Selling Coke and Pepsi Candidates," *Rake* (August 27, 2004); Chris Landers, "Consultant Profile: Bill Hillsman," *Center for Public Integrity* (September 26, 2006); Jeff Fleischer, "How to Run the Other Way," *Mother Jones* (September 13, 2004); Alexandra Staff, "Reducing the Campaign Snooze Factor," *Christian Science Monitor* (July 6, 2006); Matt Bai, "The Outlaw Strikes Again," *Newsweek* (July 9, 2000).

Special Troops: Neil Genzlinger, "The Military That Was Only for Show," *New York Times* (May 20, 2013); *The Ghost Army*, directed by Rick Beyer, PBS (2013); Megan Garber, "Ghost Army: The Inflatable Tanks That Fooled Hitler," *Atlantic* (May 22, 2013); Lynn Neary, "Artists of Battlefield Deception," National Public Radio (September 25, 2007); Cindy Cantrell, "Telling the Untold Tale of Soldiers Practiced in the Art of Deception," *Boston Globe* (February 23, 2012).

CHAPTER 10

Clint Eastwood: Scott Foundas, "Clint Eastwood: The Set Whisperer," *LA Weekly* (December 19, 2007); Robert Kapsis and Kathie

Coblentz, *Clint Eastwood: Interviews,* Oxford: University Press of Mississippi (2013); "Tough Act," *Selling Power* (July 14, 2005); Beth Marchant, "A Long, Wide Look at Eastwood's Craft," *Studio Daily* (January 22, 2013); Amy Taubin, "Interview: Clint Eastwood," *Film Comment* (January 2005).

Family Independence Initiative: Maurice Lim Miller, "Investing in Homegrown Solutions," *Huffington Post* (May 31, 2012); Maurice Lim Miller, "When Helping Doesn't Help," *Huffington Post* (May 7, 2012); Mary O'Hara, " 'Whatever We Are Doing, It Isn't Working,' " *The Guardian* (October 23, 2012); Tammerlin Drummond, "A Refreshingly Innovative Approach to Fighting Poverty," *San Jose Mercury News* (March 11, 2012); David Bornstein, "Poverty Posse," *New York Times* (July 17, 2011); Caroline Preston, "A Veteran Anti-Poverty Activist Finds a Cheaper Way to Achieve Results," *Chronicle of Higher Education* (April 18, 2010).

Trader Joe's: Jesus Sanchez, "Trader Joe's Founder Again on a Solo Path," *Los Angeles Times* (August 12, 1988); Christopher Palmeri, "Trader Joe's Recipe for Success," *Business Week* (February 20, 2008); Glenn Llopis, "Why Trader Joe's Stands Out from All the Rest in the Grocery Business," *Forbes* (September 5, 2011); Beth Kowitt, "Inside the Secret World of Trader Joe's," *Fortune* (August 23, 2010).

CONCLUSION

East Japan Railways: Christopher Carey, "Companies Are Getting an Idea That Creativity Is Worthwhile," *St. Louis Post-Dispatch* (April 20, 1998); Paul Sloane, "Every Business Problem Is an Opportunity for Innovation," *BQF Innovation* (July 9, 2011).

Endnotes/Research Studies

Chapter 1

1. D. Jansson and S. Smith, "Design Fixation," *Design Studies* 12 (1991): 3–11.
2. Ibid.
3. D. Zabelina and Michael Robinson, "Child's Play: Facilitating the Originality of Creative Output by a Priming Manipulation," *Psychology of Aesthetics, Creativity, and the Arts* 4 (2010): 57–65.

Chapter 2

1. J. Czapinski, "Negativity Bias in Psychology," *Polish Psychological Bulletin* 16 (1985): 27–44.
2. P. Brinkman, D. Coates, and R. Janoff-Bulman, "Lottery Winners and Accident Victims: Is Happiness Relative?" *Journal of Personality and Social Psychology* 36 (1978): 917–27.
3. John Gottman and Lowell Krokoff, "Marital Interaction and Satisfaction: A Longitudinal View," *Journal of Consulting and Clinical Psychology* 57 (1989): 47–52.
4. B. W. McCarthy, "Marital Style and Its Effects on Sexual Desire and Functioning," *Journal of Family Psychotherapy* 10 (1999): 1–12.

5. C. Estrada, A. M. Isen, and M. J. Young, "Positive Affect Influences Creative Problem Solving and Reported Source of Practice Satisfaction in Physicians," *Motivation and Emotion* 18 (1994): 285–99.

CHAPTER 3

1. Stanley Milgram, "Behavioral Study of Obedience," *Journal of Abnormal and Social Psychology* 67 (1963): 371–78.
2. J. Burger, "Replicating Milgram: Would People Still Obey Today," *American Psychologist* 64 (2009): 1–11.
3. M. Landau et al., "Windows into Nothingness: Terror Management, Meaninglessness, and Negative Reactions to Modern Art," *Journal of Personality and Social Psychology* 90 (2006): 879–92.

CHAPTER 4

1. Edward Deci, "Intrinsic Motivation, Extrinsic Reinforcement and Inequity," *Journal of Personality and Social Psychology* 22 (1972): 113–20.
2. E. L. Deci, "Effects of Externally Mediated Rewards on Intrinsic Motivation," *Journal of Personality and Social Psychology* 18 (1971): 105–15.
3. C. Slotterback, H. Leeman, and M. Oakes, "No Pain, No Gain: Perceptions of Calorie Expenditures of Exercise and Daily Activities," *Current Psychology* 25 (2006): 28–41.

CHAPTER 5

1. Solomon Asch, "Studies of Independence and Conformity," *Psychological Monographs* 70 (1956): 1–70.
2. M. Bazerman, A. Tenbrunsel, and K. Wade-Benzoni, "Negotiating with Yourself and Losing: Making Decisions with Competing Internal Preferences," *Academy of Management Review* 23 (1998): 225–41.
3. M. Ruef, "Strong Ties, Weak Ties and Islands: Structural and Cultural Predictors of Organizational Innovation," *Industrial and Corporate Change* 11 (2202): 427–49.

Chapter 6

1. R. Knox and J. Inkster, "Postdecision Dissonance at Post Time," *Journal of Personality and Social Psychology* 8 (1968): 319–23.
2. D. Dunning, D. Griffin, J. Milojkovic, and L. Ross, "The Over-confidence Effect in Social Prediction," *Journal of Personality and Social Psychology* 58 (1990): 568–81.
3. M. Slepian and N. Ambady, "Fluid Movement and Creativity," *Journal of Experimental Psychology: General* 141 (2012): 625–29.

Chapter 7

1. Thomas Ward, "Structured Imagination: The Role of Category Structure in Exemplar Generation," *Cognitive Psychology* 27 (1994): 1–40.
2. S. Ritter et al., "Diversifying Experiences Enhance Cognitive Flexibility," *Journal of Experimental Social Psychology* 48 (2012): 961–64.

Chapter 8

1. Walter Mischel, Yuichi Shoda, and Monica Rodriquez, "Delay of Gratification in Children," *Science* 244 (1989): 933–38.
2. Walter Mischel and Nancy Baker, "Cognitive Appraisals and Transformations in Delay Behavior," *Journal of Personality and Social Psychology* 31 (1975): 254–61.
3. O. Ayduk et al., "Regulating the Interpersonal Self: Strategic Self-Regulation for Coping with Rejection Sensitivity," *Journal of Personality and Social Psychology* 79 (2000): 776–92.
4. A. Leung et al., "Embodied Metaphors and Creative 'Acts,'" *Psychological Science* 23 (2012): 502–9.

Chapter 9

1. Albert Rothenberg, "Word Association and Creativity," *Psychological Reports* 33 (1973): 3–12.
2. Albert Rothenberg, "Opposite Responding as a Measure of Creativity," *Psychological Reports* 33 (1973): 15–18.

3. D. Romer, "Do Firms Maximize Value? Evidence from Professional Football," *Journal of Political Economy* 114: 340–65.

CHAPTER 10

1. Bibb Latané and Judith Rodin, "A Lady in Distress: Inhibiting Effects of Friends and Strangers on Bystander Intervention," *Journal of Experimental Social Psychology* 5 (1969): 189–202.
2. C. Ortner, S. Kilner, and P. Zelazo, "Mindfulness Mediation and Reduced Emotional Interference on a Cognitive Task," *Motivation and Emotion* 31 (2007): 271–83.

INDEX

INDEX